Total Quality in the Chemical Industry

Total Quality in the Chemical Industry

Edited by

G. R. Turner
Ciba-Geigy Additives, Manchester

and

J. M. Askey
Harcros Chemicals UK Ltd., Eccles

ROYAL
SOCIETY OF
CHEMISTRY

The Proceedings of a Symposium jointly organized by the North West Region of the Industrial Division of the Royal Society of Chemistry and the Society of Chemical Industry. 4–5th September 1991, University of Salford

Special Publication No. 104

ISBN 0-85186-497-X

A catalogue record of this book is available from the British Library

Published by The Royal Society of Chemistry
Thomas Graham House, Science Park, Cambridge CB4 4WF

Printed and bound in Great Britain by Bookcraft (Bath) Ltd.

Preface

The Total Quality Philosophy has become an integral part of business management within many chemical companies. The aim of this conference was to bring together the experiences of manufacturers and service suppliers and to encourage delegates to act in their own organisations. By publishing proceedings of the conference we hope to make these experiences available to a wider audience and to contribute to the momentum of quality improvement.

The papers describe a wide spectrum of experience and approach. The aim of the conference was to place emphasis on the total quality approach and in particular, with the approach of 1992, the European dimension. An insight into many aspects of Total Quality Management in the chemical industry was provided by speakers from differing sizes and types of company. Topics discussed included ISO 9000, training for success and specialist techniques.

We wish to acknowledge the work of the other members of the organising committee, namely;

> Dr D A Cornforth
> Dr G Davison
> Dr W Hoyle
> Mr A Williamson
> Mrs C Sharp

We also extend our thanks to the authors for providing their manuscripts, and to Miss C Lyall of the Royal Society of Chemistry for arranging this special publication.

This conference is the third in a series sponsored by the RSC and SCI, but the first for which proceedings have been published. We hope that this collection of papers will contribute to your own Total Quality process.

> G R Turner
> J M Askey

Contents

Introduction

The papers in this book describe experiences of implementing Total Quality Management in different situations and in different parts of the Chemical Industry. For those who are already following or setting out on the road to TQM these first hand accounts will hopefully smooth the road by pointing out potential pitfalls or useful approaches in advance.

For those to whom TQM is, as yet, little more than yet another set of initials and yet another claimed road to the promised land we attempt in this chapter to give an introduction to the background and terminology. There is now an extensive literature covering all aspects of the Quality field. The bibliography is not exhaustive but should serve as an introduction for those seeking to widen their knowledge.

The 'Total Quality' philosophy came to wide-spread prominence in British Industry in the 1980's but has a considerably longer history in other countries, notably Japan.

Traditionally in the Chemical Industry the word quality usually referred to conformance to specification. This was determined by testing of a sample of finished product in the 'QC laboratory'. Attempts to convince customers that you were a quality supplier would probably have focused on how up to date the QC testing laboratories were and, possibly, the excellent level of technical service that could be offered. This narrow definition of quality based on the inspection and servicing of products has now been expanded to cover all business activities and every factor affecting customer satisfaction. The Total Quality Philosophy is a new way of managing a business to gain maximum productivity, profitability and customer loyalty. Every aspect of the customer - supplier relationship is included in this total business approach and the mechanisms for achieving overall success through highly motivated, capable people are the keystones of TQM.

This new awareness in the UK began in earnest with the publication in 1982 of the White Paper 'Standards, Quality and International Competitiveness'. The first major focus resulting from these early initiatives was on Quality Systems and the British Standard for such systems, BS5750. The first response from the Chemical Industry was somewhat sceptical. The standards had their origin outside of the chemical industries and the terminology seemed biased to the engineering industries. However, proponents of Quality Systems maintained that they were applicable to all industries, that the terminology was of secondary importance and that the development of a formalised management system was the main goal regardless of industry. Although this principle was fairly readily accepted the terminology did lead to lengthy discussions between the BSI and several chemical companies who wanted to follow the BS5750 route. These concerns were taken up by the Chemical Industries Association and others culminating in agreement between the CIA and BSI which clarifies the application of BS5750 to the Chemical Industry. The CIA have now published a set of guidelines to ISO9001 (the international equivalent of BS5750:part 1).

Once having overcome these initial difficulties the Chemical Industry rapidly embraced BS5750 and many companies sought and achieved registration to this standard. In the true spirit of TQM however many companies have not stopped there but have used this as simply a base from which to improve.

The remainder of this chapter addresses 'Total Quality Management', 'Quality Systems' and 'Statistical Process Control' in more details.

Total Quality Management

Total Quality is an approach to managing a business in such a way that the customers are totally satisfied with the products and services they receive and this is achieved at minimum cost. In overview this is achieved by ensuring that the company is clear about the customers requirements (in all respects), that the product is designed for complete satisfaction and ease of manufacture (delivery in the case of services), that errors, failure and waste are eliminated at every stage and that the business is run in a co-ordinated fashion. Oakland in his book "Total Quality Management" proposes that total quality is structured around twelve key areas and shows in detail how to approach these:

- Understanding
- Commitment
- Organisation
- Measurement
- Planning
- Design
- System
- Capability
- Control
- Teamwork
- Training
- Implementation

A key figure in the development of total quality was Dr W E Deming, an American consultant whose work in Japan during the 1950's provided the foundation for the rise to prominence of that country's manufacturing industry. His major works are ""Quality, Productivity and Competitive Position" and "Out of the Crisis" in which he identifies 14 key aspects of management excellence:

- Create constancy of purpose for the improvement of product and service.
- Adopt the new philosophy
- Cease dependence on inspection to achieve quality
- Minimise total costs by working closely with suppliers
- Continuously improve
- Train on the job

- Adopt and institute leadership
- Drive out fear
- Break down functional barriers
- Eliminate slogans, exhortations and targets
- Eliminate numerical goals and quotas
- Eliminate the annual rating system
- Institute a program of self improvement and education
- Take action on the above points

Deming's 14 points are aimed at managers in any organisation and are designed to show them how to begin their journey towards excellence through their own actions and the way in which they deal with their people. Only Demings work with regard to measurement, process capability, design and statistical techniques is specifically product orientated.

Similar work has been developed extensively by Peters and his co-writers. Peter's original book "In search of Excellence" and his subsequent work "A Passion for Excellence" detail how companies have achieved excellence in their field by relating stories, anecdotes and research findings from them. The thrust of the work centres around the leadership qualities of the people running the operations and in this respect provides a valuable resource of practical examples of how various companies have pursued their goals. From this work the authors have distilled 8 points common to all the excellent companies in which they were involved:

- They stay close to their customers
- They stick to what they know best
- They strive for simplicity
- Strong leadership and corporate identity
- They allow and encourage entrepreneurship
- Biased towards action
- They have strong central values but allow flexibility around these
- They instil a sense of shared purpose in their employees

Subsequent work by Peters in his book "Thriving on Chaos - A Handbook for the Management Revolution" develops his previous work including his strategy of MBWA (management by wandering about) into a series of prescriptions for success.   The work of Deming and of Peters is closely related and many points of commonality can be found. Their work overlaps with that of Oakland although they concentrate on the human, organisational and customer contact aspects of the total quality approach rather than detail quality improvement techniques.

Other key writers in the field are Juran, Crosby and Schonberger (see bibliography).

It has long been accepted in western industry that higher quality goods or services inevitably incur higher costs. Crosby in his most famous book "Quality is Free" asserts that achieving zero defects actually contributes to profitability and that the historical belief that high production and high quality are incompatible is false. He also contributes a "management maturity grid" which can be used to assess a company with regard to its total quality status. Such aids can be valuable in clarifying a company's view of itself and in gaining top management commitment for taking action.

The phrase "World Class Manufacturing" was coined by Schonberger to represent the Total Quality concept. His book "Japanese Manufacturing Techniques: Nine Hidden Lessons in Simplicity" offers a view of how the Japanese have used simplification to boost their capability and his second book "World Class Manufacturing" links together many techniques, philosophies and ideas into a coherent route map for achieving manufacturing excellence. His work is equally applicable to services. The Total Quality Philosophy that Schonberger calls WCM (World Class Manufacturing) is summed up, in his opinion, by the motto of the Olympic Games "citius, altius, fortius"; "faster, higher, stronger".

Joseph Juran, like Deming, has played a major role in developing total quality over a considerable period of time. Juran also worked with the Japanese in the 1950's and can share with Deming some of the credit for that country's manufacturing success. His early but significant contribution was the "universal sequence of breakthrough" that he described in his book "Managerial Breakthrough" . This describes the mechanism of problem solving in eight key steps.

One of his other major areas of work is the concept of quality costing which is described in both his Quality Control Handbook and in Quality Planning and Analysis . Along with Crosby he shows that improved quality can lead to improved performance and reduced costs. Significant work in this area has also been reported by Dale and Plunkett (see bibliography). The key factor in the quality cost approach to TQM is the reduction of waste in the company thereby contributing directly to profitability and capability.

In summary the total quality approach has an impact in all aspects of any organisation and has been the subject of much literature. Although much of the literature is devoted to either convincing the executive that he must adopt the new philosophy or espousing a particular guru's viewpoint there are a number of more practical papers and these are well worth the industrial quality specialists attention.

British Standard 5750:Part 2:1987

BS5750 has become widely accepted by the chemical industry and many companies are now registered to the standard. Quality systems have a place in the total quality approach and the standard is discussed below.

BS 5750 is a quality system standard identical in every way to the ISO 9000 series, the international quality standard. It is made up of three parts:

- Part 1: Specification for design / development, production, installation and servicing.

- Part 2: Specification for production and installation.
- Part 3: Specification for final inspection and test.

Part 3 of the standard is a sub set of part 2 and part 2 in turn is a sub set of part 1. The uses of the standard are defined by BSI as:

Part 1: For use when conformance to specified requirements is to be assured by the supplier during several stages which may include design/development, production, installation and servicing.

Part 2: For use when conformance to specified requirements is to be assured by the supplier during production and installation.

Part 3: For use when conformance to specified requirements is to be assured by the supplier solely at final inspection and test.

In addition to publishing the standard BSI also acts as a commercial organisation in marketing BS 5750 assessment as a benefit to companies.

The history of the standard has been traced to origins in the NATO standard, "AQAPs" (Allied Quality Assurance Publications) and the British Ministry of Defence procurement standards DEF STAN 05-21 and 05-29. The 1987 revision of the standard superseded the first edition that was published in 1979.

The standard was primarily aimed at engineering component manufacturers but has since found application in many other fields. It has started to become a global trading standard despite the intense criticism that it has also attracted.

Much advice is now available on the application of the standard to a variety of industries. The official guidelines to the standard published by the British Standards institute are contained in part four of the standard (BS 5750:part 4:1990). Part four of the standard does not add any requirements to those in the other parts in the standard and is only intended as guidance to them. Part 4,1990 supersedes the previous guidance issued as Part 4,1981; part 5,1981 and part 6,1981 which have now been withdrawn.

After several years of experience with the standard guidelines specifically tailored to the needs of the chemical industry have become available. Of these the two most prominent are published by the British Chemical Distributors and Traders Association and the Chemical Industries Association . Both publications are designed for broad guidance only and make clear definitions of the technical terms relating to the application of the standard in the chemical industry before offering specific guidance.

As the use of the BS 5750 / ISO 9000 standard has spread through the industry most aspects of the issues have received thorough discussion. The standard has become part of the management tool kit. The wider European issues have also been discussed although the discussions have tended to concentrate on the administration of the assessment bodies and harmonising their standards rather than the actual practices of individual companies.

Despite the reservations expressed by some writers BS 5750 is still seen as a good minimum requirement for quality improvement and as a firm foundation for progress. In the field of Total Quality the BS5750 quality system receives little attention. However Oakland in his book "Total Quality Management" (Oakland, 1989) recognises the quality system in general as a significant element of the Total Quality approach.

Experience more directly related to the chemical industry. McCrae (1988) examines some of the issues particular to the chemical industry and attempts to guide chemical companies with regard to which part of the standard to apply. Owen (1988) and Birkinshaw (1987) relate the specific experience of a small chemical company from the view of the quality manager and managing director respectively and make particular reference to the selection of the appropriate part of the standard for use too.

In summary the quality system is widely regarded as a significant contributor to the quality effort but also one that needs to be carefully managed if it is to avoid being cumbersome and unwieldy.

Statistical Process Control

For many in the Chemical Industry their introduction to SPC will have been a request from a customer to provide "SPC data on all your products with Cpk values". For those on the technical side this may have come via someone in marketing who was very glad to be able to pass it on.

Many of these early requests came from small firms who were suppliers to some part of the automotive industry. They had been given the message that to continue to supply the large motor manufacturers they would not only have to use SPC themselves but also demonstrate that their own suppliers were doing so. Unfortunately many of the requests revealed that some of the senders knew little more, or possibly less, than the receiver. As an example I received a request for:

"SPC data on all the products you supply. (SPC = standard product control)."

These early experiences were particularly unfortunate in that they led to two very negative beliefs:

1. SPC is something you do because you have to do it.

2. SPC is about turning out specific numbers to satisfy customers who insist on having them.

Any business enterprise must add value to produce goods or services which a customer wishes to buy and for which he is prepared to pay a premium over the manufacturing cost of the goods or cost of provision of the service. The success of the enterprise will depend on the willingness of a customer to pay for the goods or service and on the premium between sales price and cost of manufacture or provision. Anything that can either increase the attractiveness of the product or service, or control the costs of production, will improve the chances of success. Given the current high level of international competitiveness and the ever increasing rate of change, dependence on experience and "feel" can no longer be relied upon for success. It is essential to have reliable means of optimising, and improving, all aspects of the production process.

SPC and other "Quality Tools" are an essential support in achieving this optimisation and improvement. It is almost certain that by using these techniques it will be possible to provide customers with information that will assist them. This must, however, be a consequence rather than the driving force. Any restrictions in application of these techniques probably lies more in lack of knowledge and imagination than in inherent limitations of the techniques themselves.

Design and development can be more reliable and cost effective by the use of experimental design and techniques such as those espoused by Taguchi and others. The techniques which have become known as the "Seven Tools" can be applied across a wide range of activity. Control of production processes, and effective use of raw materials are well known but such techniques are equally valuable in, for example, marketing, accounting and banking. The Seven Tools are described by Howard Coulson in the chapter "Application of the Total Quality Management Process in the manufacture of polymers".

It has been said that the pursuit of quality is not essential in that survival is not obligatory. As SPC techniques are a major weapon to be deployed in the search for continuous improvement, their appropriate application will be essential in any effective TQM programme. It is this context of continuous improvement which is vital to the successful application of SPC. A half-hearted implementation designed only to produce charts or figures for a customer will never reach the critical mass of enthusiasm and widespread use necessary for continued success.

SPC is a set of tools designed to help carry out certain tasks. As with many aspects of quality, the nomenclature is often far more of a hindrance than a help. Many people, perhaps with memories of sheets of calculations and formulae to calculate standard deviation, are put off by the very presence of the word statistics. A request from customer for the urgent provision of statistics, with perhaps a partially veiled threat as to what may happen if they are not provided, is not the best way to convince such people of the immense potential of such tools.

Many techniques which hail under the banner of SPC in fact use no formal statistics at all. Brainstorming, cause and effect diagrams, flow charting, Pareto analysis and other simple techniques to assist in problem solving are regularly referred to in texts on SPC. Much data in the chemical industry is collected on batch cards or similar documents and is only referred to when a problem arises. It is usually at this point that the discovery is made that a good proportion of the data have not been recorded. All that is needed to overcome this situation is to plot the data against time or batch number rather than simply recording it as numbers. Not only are any omissions immediately obvious but so are trends and deviations. If sufficient interest is shown by supervision annotation of such plots with comments referring to unusual events should follow fairly naturally. If sufficient interest is not shown by supervision then those charged with recording the data will question whether the effort is worthwhile. No one should then be surprised if some data points go unrecorded.

Control charts, once set up, can be used in the same way as any other document for recording data and for this no understanding of the background is necessary as long as there are clear instructions on what action to take if limits on the chart are exceeded. The effectiveness of any technique will be very much improved if those using it do have some understanding of the background. A knowledge of two points is sufficient:

1. The difference between random and assignable causes of variation.

2. The relationship of lines on a control chart to the distribution of random errors.

The first point is simple to convey. Most people can readily give examples of the two types of error when they have been described in relation to their own work. The second is a little more difficult but with recourse to the wide array of training material now available should not be a problem. For anyone contemplating holding a training course John Gilbert's chapter "Tidal Tactics to Total Quality" provides some excellent advice from first hand experience.

Further complications have again arisen because of difference between the chemical and other industries. The concept of taking, say, 4 samples an hour may be common practice to an engineering component manufacturing or to a pharmaceutical tableting operation. It has little relevance however to a manufacture of bulk chemicals, particularly liquids. The initial reaction in many cases was, of course, that these techniques are not relevant to manufacture of bulk liquids chemicals. This is only true to the extent that some thought and care is needed with all these techniques to ensure that they are correctly and appropriately applied in each case. A common and valuable piece of advice is that the motivating force behind applying SPC tools must be to assist in solving problems and gaining control and improvement of processes and not just in order to demonstrate use. The need to choose appropriate techniques for the types of operations which are common in the Chemical Industry was recognised by Ford. Their booklet "Statistical Process Control for Dimensionless Materials" is an excellent introduction.

There is now plenty of excellent advice and support available for those wishing to learn more about SPC. We mention some books and sources of information in the bibliography but this is by no means exhaustive.

The label "SPC" covers a wide range of tools which can play a vital part in the TQM process. The principles of application of these techniques and the background to them can be readily learned from books or training courses. The very best books and courses cannot, however, give you a step by step guide to implementation in your own situation. To the basic knowledge of the techniques must be added imagination, determination and an ability to persuade the sceptics and give confidence to those who may back off from anything that even smells of statistics or mathematics. Some aspects of implementation will not be easy but the process can be an enjoyable and, ultimately, a profitable adventure.

Bibliography / References

BS 6143, Guide to the determination and use of quality related costs, British Standards Institution, 1981.

BS 5750 (1987) parts 1,2 and 3, British Standards Institution,

BS5750 / ISO9000: 1987 A Positive Contribution to Better Business, British Standards Institution.

BS7229: 1989 British Standard Guide to Quality Systems Auditing, British Standards Institution.

Australian Standard 2561 - 1982, "Guide to the determination and use of quality costs.", Standards Association of Australia, 1982.

Birkinshaw J P, "Experiences on the road to quality management" Chemicals, pp 27-28, October 1987.

Caplan R H, Practical Approach to Quality Control, 4th Edition, Business Books, London, 1982

Crosby P B, Quality is Free - The art of making quality certain, McGraw Hill, New York, 1979.

Dale B G and Plunkett J J, Quality Costing, Chapman and Hall. London, 1991.

Davies O L and Goldsmith P L (Eds.), Statistical Methods in Research and Production, Oliver and Boyd, Edinburgh, 1972.

Deming W E, Out of the Crisis, Press Syndicate of the University of Cambridge 1986.

Duncan A J, Quality Control and Industrial Statistics, Richard Irwin, Illinois, 1974

Feigenbaum A V, Total Quality Control, Third Edition, McGraw Hill, New York, 1983.

Grant E L and Leavenworth R S, Statistical Quality Control, McGraw Hill, New York, 1980.

Hutchins D, Just in Time, Gower Technical Press, Hants., 1988.

Ishikawa K, Guide to Quality Control, Asian Productivity Association, Tokyo, 1982.

Ishikawa K, What is Total Quality Control ? The Japanese Way., Prentice Hall, Englewood Cliffs, 1985.

Juran J M, Managerial Breakthrough, McGraw Hill, 1964.

Juran J M, Quality Control Handbook, McGraw Hill, 1979. Moroney M J, Facts from Figures, Penguin 1978

Oakland J S, Statistical Process Control, Heinemann Professional Publishing, London, 1985.

Oakland J S, Total Quality Management,Heinemann Professional Publishing, London, 1989.

Owen F J, "Why quality assurance and its application in a chemical manufacturing company ?", Chemistry and Industry, pp 491-494, August 1988.

Owen F J, "Smaller operating companies plans and experience", Proceedings of Quality Assurance in the Process Industries, Institution of Chemical Engineers, September 1988.

Peters T and Austin N, A Passion for Excellence, Random House, 1985.

Peters T, Thriving on Chaos,Alfred A Knopf Inc., 1987.

Price F, Right First Time, Gower Press, 1984.

Sayle A J, "ISO 9000 - Progression or regression", Quality News, pp 50-53, 1987.

Sayle A J,"Modern Auditing", Total Quality in the Chemical Industry Conference, Royal Society of Chemistry, September 1988.

Sayle A J, Management Audits, Allan J Sayle Ltd., 2nd edition, 1988.

Schonberger R J, World Class Manufacturing, Free Press, 1986.

West A and Phillips T M, "Lets go with 5750, Experiences of Implementing BS 5750 in a Small Chemical Company.", Proceedings of Quality Assurance in the Process Industries - QA2, IChemE Symposium papers No 4, 1988.

Changing the Culture—Measuring the Progress

W. J. Bowyer

SHELL CHEMICALS UK LTD., HERONBRIDGE HOUSE, CHESTER, UK

"The fault dear Brutus, is not in our stars but in ourselves".

> - W Shakespeare   Julius Caesar

In 1979 the British Standards Institution published the standard for Quality Systems BS5750 and in 1982 the Government White Paper "Standards, Quality and International Competitiveness" set the scene for the launch of the National Quality Campaign by the Department of Trade and Industry.

In 1986, the Chemical Industries Association overcame initial scepticism about the benefit of these developments to become active in persuading member companies to adopt the new approaches. Many member companies were already taking such action but the CIA began to promote Total Quality in a vigorous way. In the ensuing five years CIA member companies have been in the forefront of UK organisations achieving certification to BS5750 (now ISO9000).

The effort spent in the UK generally and in the Chemical Industry in particular in these subjects has been tremendous. Consultancy on ISO9000 certification and on Total Quality has been a growth industry. Yet despite this 10+ years UK industry effort and 5+ years of Chemical Industry effort in particular what do we see today?

The UK economy in its deepest recession for decades, business failures at record levels and little if any sign of recovery. Our own industry is not immune from this. The effects range from sharply decreased profitability through the rescheduling and deferring of capital expenditure to cutbacks in training, plant closures and job losses. The same remedies that have been applied in the past. How far away the remedy of job cuts is from Dr Deming's outcome of the application of quality to an enterprise to give security of employment and then more employment through increased market share!

Have we embraced the quality message too late to save our industries or are we too slow, too half hearted in our approach? One thing is certain, we need to recognise the challenge. During the past twelve months the Conseil European de Federations Industries Chimique (CEFIC) has been working on guidelines to the use of ISO9001 for the European Industry. This document was published in July 1991 . It has been based largely on similar guidelines produced by the Chemical Industries Association and it is clear from working on that committee that in greater Europe there is recognition of the lead which the UK has in the understanding and application of ISO9000 and other countries are anxious to learn from us. However, their current economic performance outstrips ours. If they do use what they learn from us what future do we have unless we speed up our own improvement process?

We must not forget the improvements we have made and become despondent. In these matters it is not possible to carry out a controlled experiment and we cannot know what would have happened had all this effort not been expanded. Perhaps the recession would have been much greater and the job losses more catastrophic. It is my belief that we have changed, we have learnt and we have made progress. But it is my concern and my challenge that we have not changed fast enough or well enough and that unless we accelerate our rate of progress the future for UK industry - not excluding the Chemical Industry-is bleak. The UK must recognise the challenge facing us at the end of 1992. To provide our population with an improving living standard and to finance the infrastructure and social benefits we want we need a strong, highly competitive manufacturing industry. How else can we attain the prosperity enjoyed by our German, French and Italian friends? We must recognise, however, that we live on the western edge of a community the centre of gravity of which is moving inexorably eastward. There will be tremendous investment opportunities in the new Germany and the emerging democracies of Eastern Europe. We, in the UK, have no automatic right to investment and to attract it we must be the natural choice through exceptional performance, excellent products, excellent service, excellent response to customer needs and excellent profitability. Nothing less will do!

So why, despite all the effort, are we still suffering? As a start see what David Hutchins head of the well known Quality Consultancy David Hutchins Associates said in an article earlier this year.

"Certification to ISO9000 will not turn your organisation into a world class company. In fact any organisation which does not have procedures in place which meet ISO9000 criteria should not be in business".

Five years ago many of us did not have such procedures in place. Most of us in the Chemical Industry now do. However, the emphasis put on ISO9000 certification by Government and to a degree by ourselves, misled many of our industry leaders into equating ISO9000 certification with Total Quality. How many organisations can say truly that the process of achieving certification has radically altered the company culture? Although change is present it is not tangible, one cannot touch it and feel it.

We hear all around us that the failure of the "Quality Message" is due to lack of leadership and lack of deep understanding of true Quality among our Directors and Senior Managers. Lack of profound Knowledge in Deming's terms. As Quality professionals we are continually challenged with such comments as "we have no time", "we don't have the resources", "Quality makes for bureaucracy and slows down business". Examined move carefully these are not reasons but excuses! They are as much excuses as blaming the exchange rate, the interest rate, the Government or the Unions are excuses. The reasons for our failure are, in my view, more fundamental.

1.   We lack the desire to pursue excellence
2.   We lack the desire to be "world class"
3.   We lack any aggressive plans to become "world class"
4.   We fail to inspire our workforce

Why? Why don't we want to pursue excellence? The cult of the good loser, the translation of defeat into victory may be fundamental traits which we have reinforced with a non-competitive culture in many of our schools. The desire to protect the weak or less able from the stigma of failure is the antithesis of the pursuit of excellence. In trying to reverse this tendency we have done it in a very Western way promoting the individual rather than the team.

Why do we not wish to be "World Class"? In a recent article in The Observer the former Chairman of ICI Sir John Harvey-Jones contrasted British and German industry. He pointed out that in contrast to our perception that German industrial performance was dominated by major companies such as BASF, Volkswagen, Hoechst etc the power rests very much in the hands of the small and medium sized family firms which make up a very high proportion of their manufacturing base. These companies strive to be world leaders. He quotes a German Company which produces virtually all the industrial knitting needles for the world.

In contrast similar UK companies seem content to be the best in Bradford or Bolton - maybe in Britain. But the step to best in the world is not seen as a desirable goal perhaps because the effort required is too great or the reward insufficient.

Without a desire to become "world class" there will be no plan to
become "world class". This inevitably means that any plans for
improvement will be modest and evolutionary not radical and
revolutionary.

What about the failure to inspire the work force? Perhaps
inspiring people is just not British! However, leadership is
about creating a vision which will make people follow you and then
communicating that vision in terms which can be understood by all
involved and more importantly which appeals to them emotionally
rather than intellectually.

Statements of the "Company Quality Policy" by now abound in the
Boardrooms, reception areas and offices of the land. But how many
of them tug at the heart strings? If the managers and the quality
professionals don't feel turned on by them how much effect are they
likely to have on the operator or the sales clerk? The Japanese sell
their intentions to the work force in a much more forthright way.
Witness Canons "Beat Xerox" slogan or "Encircle Caterpillar" as the
plan for Komatsu. The project which Toyota launched to get itself
into the luxury sports car market was called "The Porsche Killer".
How long before our Resins Business will adopt the slogan "Sink
Ciba-Geigy"?

How can we begin to change all this? In Shell Chemicals UK Ltd we
have embarked on an experiment to try and accelerate the improvement
process.

In late 1990 our Directors were persuaded to examine the
criteria contained in the American Malcolm Baldrige National
Quality Award. This award was established in 1987 by the
United States Congress in memory of Secretary of Commerce
Malcolm Baldrige. Its aims are:

*   to recognise companies that attain pre-eminent quality
        leadership

*   to develop and publicise award criteria to serve as quality
        improvement guidelines

*   to disseminate information about the quality strategies of
        Award recipients

There are three eligibility categories

*   Manufacturing Companies

*   Service companies

*   Small businesses of less than 500 employees

Two awards may be given in each category each year. The winners so far have been.

1990
Cadillac Motor Car Division (General Motors)
IBM Rochester (International Business Machines)
Federal Express Corporation
Wallace Company Inc

1989
Milliken & Co
Xerox Business Products and Systems

1988
Motorola Inc
Commercial Nuclear Fuel Division (Westinghouse)
Globe Metallurgical

The award covers seven categories with a total points score available of 1000 points. The categories and scoring system (1991 Award) are:-

1.0	Leadership	100
2.0	Information and Analysis	70
3.0	Strategic Quality Planning	60
4.0	Human Resource Utilisation	150
5.0	Quality Assurance of Products and Services	140
6.0	Quality Results	180
7.0	Customer Satisfaction	300
	TOTAL	**1000**

Within the seven categories there are thirty two separate items. For example category 7.0 Customer Satisfaction is subdivided as follows:

Category 7.0 Customer Satisfaction

Item		
Item 7.1	Determining Customer Requirements and Expectations
7.2	Customer Relationship Management
7.3	Customer Service Standards
7.4	Commitment to Customers
7.5	Complaint Resolution for Quality Improvement
7.6	Determining Customer Satisfaction
7.7	Customer Satisfaction Results
7.8	Customer Satisfaction Comparison

Each item is further subdivided into areas to address of which there are 99 in total.

It is important to note however that the categories are not independent. Their relationship is expressed in Figure: 1.0

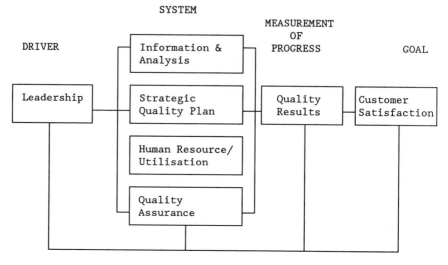

FIGURE 1.0

The task of carrying out this assessment was given to a group of
young graduates as a project within a training programme designed
to lead to a Diploma in Business Administration. At that time
there was little help available in the UK with respect to training
either in the Malcolm Baldrige criteria or in the methods of self
assessment. The team therefore, studied the criteria, devised a
comprehensive questionnaire and carried out a series of interviews
across the company. The time available did not allow every business
or every department to be covered but the sample taken was considered
to be representative of the company as a whole.

The team prepared and submitted their report in March 1991.
They did have fears that their findings might be rejected
since they had not scored the company highly. In fact the
highest score was in Section 5.0 Quality Assurance of Products
and Services. Not surprisingly considering the effort that
had been expended over the past five years.

Once they had overcome their initial shock at the low score
the Board debated and considered the findings. Far from
rejecting the report the Board recognised it as a useful and
valuable diagnosis of some of the problems associated with
the quest for quality. In this debate the performance of
genuine applications for the Malcolm Baldrige Award showed
that the sort of score we had attained put us in pretty good
company. Figure 2.0 shows the distribution of scores of the 97
companies which in 1990 were confident enough to apply for the
award. Only 12 qualified for a site visit.

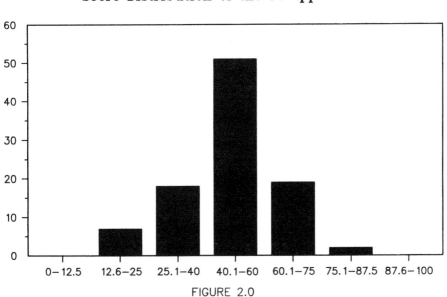

MALCOLM BALDRIGE NATIONAL QUALITY AWARD 1990

Score Distribution of the 97 Applicants

FIGURE 2.0

Added to the fact that experience indicates that self assessment tends to harder judgement than third party assessment the Board accepted that:-

*   the absolute score level is immaterial
*   the American experience puts us in good company
*   we had work to do to become a "true TQM company"

The next question, given that the Board agreed to take the action necessary to raise our performance, was what should that action be? By a fortunate co-incidence the Shell Chemicals UK Board comprises seven members. Each member has taken on responsibility for one of the seven Baldrige categories as the chairman of a small team. These seven teams are made up of five additional members representing the two manufacturing sites, the two Business Directorships and an appropriate functional representative. This team membership is designed to weld together the separate identities of the Head Office and the sites into a common Shell Chemicals UK approach. The leadership team is the Board itself and in this case fulfils two functions, that of addressing the criteria contained in the leadership section of the award and also that of co-ordinating the other six teams. These teams are set up and are beginning the

tremendous task before them. The goal however is clear. To
be a true quality company in terms of measuring up to the
Baldrige criteria means achieving a score greater than 80%.
That is the benchmark. From our internal assessment we have
identified the gap we need to close. Through this use of the
Baldrige criteria as a spur to improvement we have laid out a
corporate quality plan in overall terms. This plan can be seen
in overview in Figure 3.0.

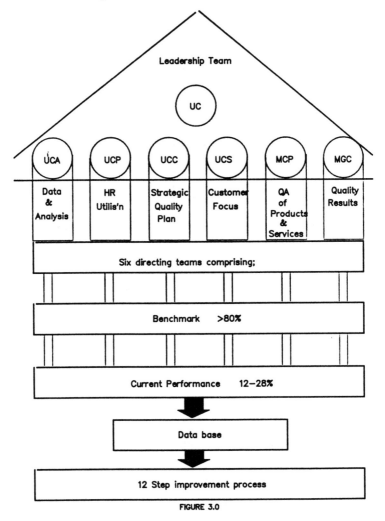

FIGURE 3.0

However, having a plan is only the start and to score highly the approach developed in the plan must be deployed throughout the organisation and results achieved. These results being related to the deployed quality plan and not by other means. The scoring method is outlined in Figure 4.0.

1991 MBNQA Scoring Guidelines "Green Sheet"

Score	Approach	Deployment	Results
0%	• anecdotal, no system evident	• anecdotal	• anecdotal
10-40%	• beginning of systematic prevention basis	• some to many major areas of business	• some positive trends in the areas deployed
50%	• sound, systematic prevention that include evaluation /improvement cycles • some evidence of integration	• most major areas of business • some support areas	• positive trends in most major areas • some evidence that results are caused by approach
60-90%	• sound, systematic prevention basis with evidence of refinement through evaluation/ improvement cycles • good integration	• major areas of business • from some to many support areas	• good to excellent in major areas • positive trends - - from some to many support areas • evidence that results are caused by approach
100%	• sound, systematic prevention basis refined through evaluation/improvement cycles • excellent integration	• major areas and support areas • all operations	• excellent (world class) results in major areas • good to excellent in support areas • sustained results • results clearly caused by approach

Figure 4.0

So far the knowledge of the Baldrige Criteria and the work done in assessing the company is known to a relatively small proportion of the total work force. Even many of the selected team members have minimal knowledge of the criteria. Thus two of the first tasks are:

Communications

-    What the Malcolm Baldrige National Quality Award is

-    What we have found in Shell Chemicals

-    What we intend to do

and Education

Team members must:-

*   Understand the criteria
*   Understand the implications
*   Appreciate the work load
*   Co-ordinate their activities

Taking this approach there are several advantages as we see it.

*   It takes the company well beyond ISO9000 whilst putting
     all the effort spent in obtaining certification into a
     deeper context

*   It provides a clear focus for the organisation

*   It has been accepted at the highest level in the Company
     and the Directors themselves are involved in achieving
     the goal

*   It forces senior management to educate themselves and be
     educated in the quality philosophy and processes

*   Use of the team approach binds the different sites and
     functions together

*   By taking a cross-section of staff into the teams the
     views of employees other than senior managers will be
     heard

*   It allows other existing initiatives to be incorporated
     in the plan

Despite all this progress it is unlikely to be plain sailing.
Potential hazards along the route include:

*   the temptation to go for quick results

*   the long time frame involved and the difficulty of
     sustaining the effort

*   the time involvement of staff required

*   it could be seen as yet another separate initiative

*   staff continuity on teams may be difficult to achieve

*   new board members may not support it

*   the training burden may be too high

The essentials of the plan lie in the operation and co-ordination of the seven teams. We have though created an eighth team. Each team has a facilitator or coach. These facilitators are full time "Quality Personnel" with good knowledge of TQM and the tools and techniques of quality. Additionally they are versed in Team Dynamics and increasingly in the understanding of the Malcolm Baldrige Award. This group must network, provide consistency of approach and give mutual support. It is this team which at least in the initial phases will have to take responsibility to keep the show on the road. In particular the facilitator will have to work very closely with the Director in his role as team chairman.

Once embarked on the process we will need to measure our progress in some way. The importance of measurement in Total Quality Management is stressed by all the experts and practitioners but a high proportion of these emphasise the measurement of 'Cost of Non-Quality' as the key which opens the minds of senior management. Unfortunately large financial rewards from the pursuit of TQM do not come in the short term and as we see in the present economic climate can be masked or eliminated by the forces of the market place. Senior managers already have plenty of financial information and if we are to change the culture we need to give them measures which are more process than results orientated. Measurement features strongly in the Baldrige criteria and does so in two distinct ways. In categories 5.0 and 6.0 the emphasis is on internal measures particularly key operating measures such as plant reliability, rework reduction etc and supplier performance. These categories also strongly emphasise benchmarking performance against world class companies. The second aspect of measurement is through customer satisfaction. Neither of these approaches demands money values although naturally costs may well be a valid measure for some aspects.

The other key measure of progress is of course to evaluate the company periodically against the Baldrige criteria and use that evaluation to direct the effort. Scoring against the criteria is not an easy task. It is time consuming and requires training. It also requires the organisation, even if using the criteria only for internal purposes, to write an application for the award. This document once established can be updated relatively simply each year and used as the basis for assessment. Ideally this assessment should be carried out by the Board but at the very least by a group of employees who are not the writers.

Winning the award is not the objective of the exercise. The objective is to improve the company's performance and it is important to make that clear to the organisation.

Nevertheless, at some point, it is quite valid to seek external recognition. UK based companies cannot compete for the Baldrige Award but in 1992 the European Quality Award sponsored by the European Foundation for Quality Management will be launched. It is to be hoped that it quickly achieves the status of the Deming Prize and the Malcolm Baldrige Award.

What we are doing in Shell Chemicals UK Ltd is not unique,
recent trade press articles show that many companies are
following a similar process. However, we believe that what
we are doing will help us address and overcome some of the
problems we are encountering in moving our quality drive
forward. It provides a focus for the organisation and
through a commitment to go for the European Quality
Award can fire the enthusiasm of the work force. It forces
management participation and education and through the
benchmarking requirements built in, it forces us to seek to be
world class.

Total Quality Management in Europe and E.F.Q.M.

Kees J. van Ham

EUROPEAN FOUNDATION FOR QUALITY MANAGEMENT, FELLENOORD 47A, 5612 AA
EINDHOVEN, THE NETHERLANDS

TQM In Europe

Companies which lead competition in the world's markets have
redefined their quality strategies and have implemented
comprehensive corporate programmes for planning, monitoring and
improving Total Quality.

Today, Total Quality Management has become a strategic priority
for business firms around the world, because of its proven
significance for acquiring and maintaining competitive advantage.
TQM is now recognised by a growing number of enterprises as the
most powerful competitive weapon.

They have come to the conclusion that the traditional sources of
competitive advantage are losing effectiveness. Conventional
single focus strategies as "Product/service differentiation",
"Cost leadership" and "Market/distribution power" are becoming
insufficient for maintaining business leadership. (reference 1).

Research shows (reference 2) that businesses that rank high in
customer-perceived quality, perform significantly better in the
marketplace than businesses whose quality is perceived as being
low.

Customer perceived Total Quality is the key to success in the
market place, and businesses would add "At the lowest consumption
of resources".

The reality of business life is now also understood by a growing
number of European Top Managers. They not only manage for
achieving Total Quality in their own companies, but have also
understood that Quality must become Europe's number one societal
value.

Customer-perceived Total Quality largely exceeds quality system
certification, still a high priority objective in many industrial
branches in Europe. More and more companies, but also supporting
organisations, like Government institutions, professional
organisations, consultants and Universities, understand the
essential but relative significance of quality system
certification. ISO 9000 and EN 29000 certification have been end
objectives in the past, but are now seen just as a foundation
stone in the journey to Total Quality.

European top management views

At the European Quality Management Forum in London on 25 October
1990, Carlo de Benedetti, Chairman and Chief Executive Officer of
Ing. C. Olivetti and C., stated: "In Olivetti, customer
satisfaction is now the only yardstick of quality" (reference 3).

Karel Vinck, Chief Executive Officer of the Bekaert Group, and
winner of the 1990 European Quality Award for Leadership in Total
Quality Management also stresses that TQM is essential for making
the company competitive in the international market. Talking
about Bekaert's approach, he states: "I worked first on
developing a Beliefs and Mission Statement for our Group. Then I
looked for a vehicle to achieve that Beliefs and Mission
Statement, and ultimately to realise the Group's strategy. I
gradually convinced myself that TQM was the best vehicle and the
best way to do this" (reference 4).

In 1989 McKinsey & company carried out a research project aiming
"To pull together top-management views on quality performance and
management of quality practices in leading European business
organisations" (reference 1).

Part of the research was done by a survey among the Chief
Executive officers of the European top 500 companies.

Some of the results of the survey are:

-   Over 90% of the CEO's consider Quality performance to be
    critical to their corporation's overall competitiveness. Over
    55% stated that it was "absolutely" critical to their
    corporation's success.

-   More than 85% of the CEO's responding, consider the management
    of Quality to be one of the top priorities, or the only top
    priority for their company. 16% said that it was seen as the
    single top corporate priority.

One of the conclusions of the McKinsey study was that "Quality
and the Management of Quality are already playing, and will
increasingly play, a renewed central role in determining
competitive performance among both global and local players".

The progress made

Several European countries have a positive quality image. This is, for instance, mentioned by the World Competitiveness Reports of 1989 and 1990. To a large extent the positive image is based upon superior craftsmanship, technological excellence or product exclusiveness.

External reports on tangible results achieved through a successful implementation of TQM in European companies are still scarce. Some statements on progress were made at events organised by E.F.Q.M.

Edmond Pachura, Chief Executive Officer of Sollac, states that Total Quality Management has been a major factor in improving his company's financial results from -1.6% in 1986 to +23.1% in 1989 (reference 5).

T. Megarbane, General Manager of Sodexho France reports that TQM in his company has led to results such as: "Higher retention of clients rate, improved productivity and financial gains" (reference 5).

A. Scharp, President and CEO of Electrolux, mentions many results from his company's Quality Programme. Amongst those are also results in the administrative area, such as improved reporting of financial results, and a reduction of overdue in accounts receivable (reference 6).

There is not yet a quantitative analysis of customer perceived improvements for European business as a whole. The introduction of the European Quality Company Award in 1992 is expected to lead, amongst many other things, to much better insight into what really has been achieved.

Some critical remarks about progress were made by J. Foden, Group Chairman and Chief Executive, PA Consulting Group, at the occasion of the London Quality Management Forum.

He reports from PA research by saying: "TQM has stagnated in many organisations. In some cases, organisations which thought they were well up the wall of quality are sliding back down it". Talking about possible reasons for a lack of success, he states: "...let's remember its only in the last few years that Europe has really taken quality seriously. Most of us have started TQM during the last 5 years and few of us can say that quality does not still need a separate push, a special push, a new initiative. We can't say it is ingrained and part of our business" (reference 3).

Europe, the United States of America and Japan

Starting in the early fifties, captains of Japan's industry turned Quality into a strategic weapon.

Some companies in the USA and Europe followed a similar path, but the Japanese promoted quality at all levels. Behind the promotion was the Japanese Union of Scientists and Engineers, in co-operation with business, Government and Universities. They set up courses, offered consultation, employed broadcasting and used the Deming Application Prize to good effect. Quality awareness and quality mindedness pervaded the country's infrastructure, both on a national and a regional level, helping Japan to create its own national quality movement.

It is only since the end of the seventies that quality has become a strategic issue for some American companies and is seen as the road to competitive advantage.

The strategic approach to quality is closely linked to business objectives, market share and financial results. It is also more sensitive to competitive performance and the customer's point of view, and more firmly anchored in the company's business processes and the total organisation.

In the United States of America, Quality is now a National issue as demonstrated by National Quality Month, National Quality Forum and the Malcolm Baldrige National Quality Award.

American business leaders take initiatives to support the introduction of Total Quality in the American infrastructure, in particular in the education system and Government organisations.

In Europe, Quality Management is not yet a total societal strategy. The first examples of European companies introducing TQM as a corporate strategy, date from the early eighties.

Many European companies are still importing Quality Management professionalism, using consultants and educational material from Japan and the USA. Very little original European research supports companies in their efforts.

But the need to look abroad is somewhat diminishing. In some European countries, Governments sponsor National campaigns, some Universities and Business schools are becoming more committed to TQM Education and Research, professional quality organisations and management associations are deploying activities and European consultancy in TQM is gaining strength.

But the breakthrough still has to come.

TQM in Europe and E.F.Q.M.

Experiences had unambiguously indicated that the development of TQM as a European value and capability is impossible without inspiring and personal leadership provided by the Senior Management of business companies.

Business organisations, more than any other group from society, understand the nature and intensity of world competition.

Many of them have the opportunity to learn directly from business relations in other parts of the world. Excellence, best in class and world leadership do have a meaning for them.

It is understandable that European business leaders took the initiative to start a Europe-wide Total Quality action and created E.F.Q.M. as an instrument to stimulate, support and create conditions.

The Presidents of E.F.Q.M.'s Founding and Key members assembled at Montreux on 19 October 1989, signed the E.F.Q.M. Policy document stating that: "Together we want to make E.F.Q.M. a strong driving force to enhance the competitive position of Western European companies in the world market. We want to combine experience, resources and forces to create conditions for making quality Western Europe's highest business objective" (reference 7).

The following Missions were defined:

- ...to support the management of Western Europe companies in accelerating the process of making quality a decisive influence for achieving global competitive advantage.

- ...to stimulate and, where necessary, to assist all segments of the Western European community to participate in quality improvement activities and to enhance the quality culture.

By now, almost 150 Western European organisations, most of them business companies, from both the industrial and the service area, have joined E.F.Q.M.

The Presidents or highest executives of all E.F.Q.M. members have explicitly subscribed to E.F.Q.M.'s Mission and Vision statements. Most Western European countries and business sectors are represented. Many Universities and Business schools have also joined. Links with the Commission of the European communities are becoming stronger. Partnerships with other European organisations either already exist or will be forged in the near future.

The outlines of E.F.Q.M.'s strategy for the coming years are taking shape and will be discussed intensively later this year with its main and most powerful support group: the Presidents and Senior Executives of its members.

E.F.Q.M.'s focus

In the coming years E.F.Q.M. will focus its activities on two main areas. These are: Recognition and Education, Training and Research.

The first priority in the Recognition programme is the implementation of the European Quality Company Award.

To win an Award, a company must demonstrate that its approach to Total Quality Management has contributed significantly to achieving benefits of value to its customers, its employees, other key stakeholders in the company and society in general.

The definition of criteria is now in its last phase. The final approval will be done by the Presidents of E.F.Q.M.'s members.

A brochure describing the criteria and main aspects of the assessment process will be published in June. The first Awards will be presented during the European Quality Management Forum in Madrid in October 1992.

The first objective in creating the European Quality Company Award is not so much to single out excellent and exemplary companies, but to introduce a European Quality Management model that can serve companies as a guide for self appraisal and educational institutes as a reference for their education and research activities.

Over 200 managers and quality professionals from the European scene have been involved in designing the Award. It may be expected that the European Quality Company Award will lead to a harmonisation of Quality Awards at all European levels. In addition to the European Quality Company Award, E.F.Q.M. continues this year with Awards for the best Thesis (both at the Doctoral and the Masters level), the best Media product on TQM and the Award for Leadership in Total Quality Management.

The Education, Training and Research activities aim at closing the gap between what companies need and Universities and Business schools have to offer.

Supported by the EC COMETT II programme, E.F.Q.M. has started a University-Enterprise Training Partnership, in addition to already existing TQM oriented UETP's of a more limited scope.

The E.F.Q.M.-led UETP will create a focus for European University-Enterprise co-operation and will manage a vast array of activities to raise the European practice of TQM related Education, Training and Research.

In addition to the UETP activity, but closely linked to it, E.F.Q.M. will stimulate, develop and manage a programme of European TQM Research which will involve Educational institutes, companies, Research institutes and sponsoring organisations all over Europe. Supported by a grant from the EC SPRINT programme, E.F.Q.M. has started to organise a series of TQM Research exchange meetings between companies and researchers.

A start has also been made to build a data bank on existing in-company Education and Training modules, including information on the conditions for availability. This data bank will facilitate exchange of material and know how between companies.

Survival and the educational infrastructure

The European TQM movement finds its roots in the need and determination of European business to survive from world competition.

European companies are more and more aware of the issues involved in a process of company-wide, long term, cultural change, and take measures to improve their capabilities.

They also understand that they need support from the European environment, and in particular from the world of Education, Training and Research.

They want to contribute, individually and collectively to building a European, TQM dedicated, educational infrastructure.

References

1. "Management of Quality: The single most important challenge for Europe"; F.W. Huibregtsen; Director McKinsey and Company; Speech delivered during the plenary session of the European Quality Management Forum at Montreux on 19 October 1989.

2. "Quality as a strategic weapon; Measuring relative quality, value, and market differentiation"; Bob Luchs; Director PIMS; The European Business Journal; Issue 4, 1990.

3. "Speeches delivered during the plenary session of the European Quality Management Forum in London on 25 October 1990"; European Foundation for Quality Management; 1991.

4. "Leadership Award winner says thanks to the Bekaert community"; Quality Link November/December 1990; European Foundation for Quality Management.

5. Proceedings of the European Quality Management Forum, 24 and 25 October 1990, London; European Foundation for Quality Management; 1990.

6. Speeches delivered during the plenary session of the European Quality Management Forum at Montreux on 19 October 1989; European Foundation for Quality Management; 1990.

7. E.F.Q.M. Policy Document; European Foundation for Quality Management; 1989.

The TQM Programme of Hoechst in the UK

D. K. Taylor

HOECHST UK LTD., HOECHST HOUSE, SALISBURY ROAD, HOUNSLOW, MIDDLESEX TW4 6JH, UK

The business activity of Hoechst in the U.K. concerns an exceptionally wide range of products and markets and the company operates at a large number of sites in the country. The manufacturing base is at present not large but is growing and, as the wholly owned subsidiary of Hoechst A.G., the majority of products and services of the parent company are represented in the U.K. in sales and marketing terms. Implementing a total quality programme therefore involved a large number of employees, widely spread and from a wide variety of disciplines and work functions.

The Hoechst U.K. T.Q.M. programme is very nearly two years old and it is relevant to consider why the programme was considered necessary, how it was implemented and to comment on the present status.

In the recent past an increasing number of customers who were applying for registration to the relevant part of BS5750 needed verification that Hoechst was an "approved source" and needed statements that products supplied were to specification i.e. statements of conformity. Because so many of the supplying works of Hoechst A.G. were registered to ISO9000, or seeking registration, it was a fairly straight forward procedure to demonstrate that Hoechst was an approved source. Similarly the preparation and issue of statements of conformity was not difficult although it became an onerous task.

The need to provide both types of information increased very significantly. Moreover, providing the information was no guarantee that the business was secure – competition was, and still is, just as intense and all that was changing was an increase in customer's expectations and a sharper focus on supplier performance.

Parallel with that activity were two additional dimensions. Firstly an increasing tendency for unsolicited vendor ratings by which Hoechst was assessed as a supplier against a number of criteria of which product quality in itself played a relatively minor part but in which service quality predominated. Secondly the steady increase in the international flavour of the U.K. market, especially for industrial products, and the ability of competitors from as far away as the Far East to achieve demanding delivery schedules and to maintain a highly satisfactory after-sales service.

What all of this began to show clearly was that product quality was just as important, but so was the quality of the service that went with it. It was not enough to point to research expenditure or new product developments, the customers' specification meant product quality and service quality and a continuity of both. This was achievable but only by adopting the key principles of the management of total quality.

A programme was begun that focused on fulfilling the needs of customers - all customers, not only those external organisations to whom products were sold and marketed but also internal customers i.e. colleagues within the organisation to whom or from whom a variety of services were supplied. Not only was the programme aimed at each and every employee it was also far-reaching in concept and structure. It could have been implemented using in-house training resources which would have been considerably stretched however and it was felt that credibility would be better ensured if outside expertise were used. A number of T.Q.M. consultants were approached and subsequently vetted and a relatively small firm selected on the basis of their clear and concise presentation of total quality principles coupled with very extensive management experience from within manufacturing industry. The consultants who were to play an active role in the eventual training programme visited each of the main sites of Hoechst in the U.K. and had detailed discussions with personnel representing key functions to establish perceptions of the quality of service provided at that time to both internal and external customers. This invaluable information was used to tailor the T.Q.M. programme to the particular needs of the company.

The programme that evolved was implemented in three phases the first of which concerned all directors and senior managers of the company who each attended a one and a half day training module every month for five months. The main subjects considered were:-

        - Listening to Customers
        - Customer Focused Innovation
        - Measuring and Controlling Quality and Service
        - Foundations of Quality and Service
        - Achieving Excellent Quality and Service

Attendance by the nominated personnel was mandatory,

the sessions were designed to be highly participative and specific follow-up actions relating the principles learned to actual working environments were implemented between each module.

Towards the end of the first phase individual trainers or focal points had been identified for each department or site who had been participants in the first phase and who had the responsibility to "cascade" the process to the next layer of management or supervision. In this, the second phase, a further series of training sessions were undertaken for larger groups of personnel and were designed to suit the specific needs of the business unit, site or service department. The number and frequency of such sessions varied accordingly but all were completed within four months.

The third phase was a logical extension of the cascade process in that all remaining personnel received "customer awareness" training and training in specific skills was organised where relevant and appropriate. This phase is on-going in that refresher training is organised to reinforce the principles of T.Q.M., particularly for new employees, and every training course irrespective of its subject and content has been modified to encompass T.Q.M. in the widest sense.

Just before the first phase began an important measurement was made of the current perception by customers of the quality of service provided by Hoechst in the U.K. This benchmark was obtained with the aid of a questionaire sent to 20 per cent of all customers computer-selected at random. Each customer was asked to rate service quality in four criteria - Communications, Distribution, Products and Systems on a 1 to 10 scale - 1 being Poor and 10 Excellent. The questionaires were aimed at the customers of each major business area of the company, the response rate was encouragingly high and although the results showed some variation the company average was almost 7 - an equally encouraging starting point. The complete exercise is being repeated now to see where the effects of implementing T.Q.M. have been particularly beneficial and where some remedial action may be necessary.

To a large extent the implementation of a far-reaching and comprehensive T.Q.M. programme in Hoechst in the U.K. has meant changing the culture of the organisation and the attitude of employees. The management of total quality is genuinely a journey not a destination and since the programme is barely two years old it could be said that the journey has only just begun. Much has been achieved already which is testimony not only to the quality of the training material and expertise from the external consultants but also to the enthusiasm and commitment of the key individuals charged with implementing total quality in their respective areas of responsibility. The essential features of T.Q.M. have been embodied in a mission statement with which every employee has become familiar and which is extensively publicised throughout the company. The statement is based on four so-called guiding principles which are:-

- Hoechst U.K. is committed to creating long term customer satisfaction - by providing high quality products and outstanding customer service.

- All employees will continually strive for excellence in the quality of their work and will establish close, effective and long-lasting working partnerships with Hoechst A.G. and other suppliers, and their colleagues within Hoechst U.K., in pursuit of this goal.

- The company will always respect the environment in which it operates and will endeavour to play its part as a responsible member of the community.

- Hoechst U.K. will continue to improve its profitability through the careful control of all its activities within these principles, thus providing opportunities and long-term security for its customers, suppliers and employees.

Even at this early stage of the T.Q.M. journey in Hoechst in the U.K. the results are both positive and measurable. The fact that the programme has been successful depends on a number of factors the most important of which are listed below as advisory recommendations to any organisation keen to tread a similar path:-

- Commitment of Chief Executive
- Commitment and active participation of Directors and Senior Management
- Selection of appropriate consultant given freedom to act
- Appointment of senior focal point with authority
- Involvement of all personnel
- Make it enjoyable
- Quickly identify positive results and publicise them
- Keep the momentum going: T.Q.M. is a journey not a destination

Finally what significant lessons have been learned? Firstly that an ambitious programme such as this is a dimension of "change management", any substantial change in working practices requires committed champions of the cause. Selection and appointment of these, especially in the more sensitive parts of an organisation, can be a critical success factor in eradicating cynicism and scepticism and potential "not invented here" problems.

Secondly in the formative stages of any T.Q.M. programme a natural consequence is to establish working practice, study groups, quality circles, committees and the like the remit of which is to determine and define various action plans. Desirable and commendable though this work is, there is an inherent danger that as the T.Q.M. programme matures the work of such groups continues parallel to but <u>separate</u> from normal day to day working practice. This can be counter-productive - the activity of any organisation is a fabric in which the management of total quality should be an endless thread.

Tidal Tactics to Total Quality

John Gilbert

AKZO CHEMICALS LTD., HOLLINGWORTH ROAD, LITTLEBOROUGH, LANCASHIRE OL15 0BA, UK

1. INTRODUCTION

More than a year of experience with a Total Quality (TQ) process, shows clearly that the courageous decision to adopt TQ in Akzo Chemicals will result in many changes and greatly benefit our customers, employees, and shareholders. TQ know no barriers; geographical, cultural or linguistic and can help large organisations to simultaneously adopt both a global and local parentage no longer dominated by any single nation or region. For the European arm of Akzo Chemicals,

Total Quality = Common Culture = European

I have been taught the principles of TQ and many of the nuts and bolts required to make it work and spent much of my time organising and teaching the process principles to my colleagues in 3-day workshops.

This paper is mainly about a few practical examples of what to do and what not to do when implementing a customer focused quality improvement process. The process of institutionalising Total Quality within an organisation can be compared with the half-cycle of a tide ebbing and flowing. For every two steps forward, a step back can be taken if the details of decisions and actions are carried out imperfectly.

The definition of quality has been expressed in many ways, but in any one organisation, quality can only be defined in one way. In Akzo Chemicals, we define quality as **Consistent conformance to customers' expectation.** Whatever definition you use, be sure that everyone knows exactly what it means and hammer the definition relentlessly into your organisation.

Observing the favourable reactions of the participants of our Total Quality workshops, where these principles were taught, gives those of us responsible for the process implementation, the enthusiasm to continue along this long hard road.

2. WORKSHOP EXPERIENCES

The people arrive in groups of 25 from all over the UK and abroad. They are the managers, office staff, factory personnel, supervisors, sales people and directors. They are a mix of ages, attitudes, disciplines and seniority. They come cheerfully but not from choice. They come because our president committed them to come. He committed 8000 of us to spend a few days each to learn the principles of TQ.

Some arrive feeling they had better things to do, all are curious and most are open-minded, willing for a few days to give this latest 'project' the benefit of the doubt and then return to the old ways. None expect TQ to change them.

The workshop participants learn many basic principles, how to identify, analyse and solve problems in small and large teams and the guiding principle that TQ is simply conforming to customers' expectations. They learn that if they never deal personally with the customers who buy our products and services, they *still* have customers of their own, their internal customers; their peers, their bosses and those they supervise.

They learn that discovering what customers expect means - you ask them, and that error prevention is preferable to time consuming error correction. These are disturbing concepts and some participants admit they will never be the same again.

They learn that TQ is the continuous, never ending process of running an enterprise with the intention of doing things right the first time every time, an intention based on understanding customer expectations and then complying with them.

Most of them do not get out of bed each day simply for the money, they do it because they care about their work and feel decently obligated to earn their pay. They are good quality people and would rather do a good job than a bad one. Most of them are doing the best they can, faced often with demeaning rules and barriers erected by others. They learn that these rules and barriers will be demolished and management admits the presence of these imperfections and is leading the way to an improved future.

They ask why we, their colleagues, are teaching TQ? Why not a consultant who could say it so much more prettily? We explain that a consultant cannot put TQ in place, he can only teach us the common sense TQ model and the tools. The rest we must do ourselves.

They learn that TQ is not an experiment; it empowers both decision-making at lower levels and their right to demand a coherent answer to their questions. They learn how to develop a customer-supplier relationship with their staff, but that TQ is not utopia. Sometimes decisions are made which people dislike, but the decisions must be properly explained. They show a gradual realisation that as people begin to pull together in the same direction, adversarial relationships diminish and the natural competition among people is channelled into more productive directions.

They learn that TQ does not seek to change their personal culture, but leads them, through training, to better procedures which allows them to do their job their way. It helps to build pride and even loyalty. Everybody is loyal to something; family, friend, union, company. TQ helps to share the loyalty out more.

The workshops help to find many patient and diplomatic evangelists who 'infect' the organisation with attitudes which start 'improvement'. Gradually, others are infected by the 'virus' and the improvements spread. But it is unrealistic to expect people to remain committed only to beautifully composed rhetoric. The commitment comes from seeing the organisation get better. Therefore, the improvements must be measured and relentlessly communicated.

When TQ has built the commitment of the organisation's people to the recognition of the benefits of cooperation and sharing, and the skills needed are developed through training, their diverse untapped talents really begin to be used.

They leave the workshops as potential new-team members, a few are even enthusiastic and elated because TQ is a management stimulated release of the commitment which most of them felt anyway. Many are disturbed to discover that the 'project' is a 'process', with no finishing date; it's permanent, it will not go away. Others are confused but comforted to know that the apparently abstract concepts of TQ will become a concrete process they can learn and apply like any other part of strategic planning.

3. WORKSHOP ORGANISATION

The work involved in running a smoothly organised workshop is considerable. Even before the workshop starts, there are many activities which must be carefully thought out in order that participants arrive in the best frame of mind and with enough curiosity aroused to encourage an open-minded attitude.

We ran our workshops like a military campaign. We used a check-list of items to be addressed, from the workshop inventory (600 individual items), video tapes wound to the correct place, mints and glasses on the tables, and so on....

It is impossible here to describe more than just a few of the scores of issues which should be addressed. However, we hope you will get a flavour of the care and attention which is necessary to run successful workshops where each participant is treated as an individual about whom you must care because he or she is important to the success of your Total Quality Process.

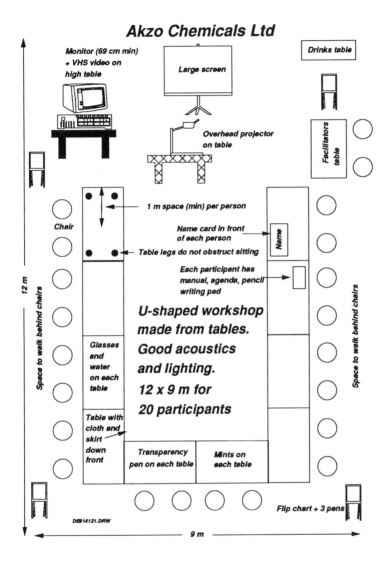

Workshop Layout

4. TIDAL TACTICS EXAMPLES

① **Workshop Introduction**

Send each participant an individual letter from top management well before the workshop is due to start detailing why they are 'requested' to attend, when, for how long, how to get there, a list of other participants, the hotel arrangements and even the options on dress. Most people do not travel on business a great deal and need to know if dress will be suit and tie or in our case *'smart but casual'*.

Message. By ensuring that people know precisely what will happen when they arrive at the workshop, the reason for their presence and who else will be there, their confidence is increased and they will learn and accept more of what is taught to them.

② **Seating Arrangements**

The participants sit around a U-shaped table. We spent lots of time arranging the seating places to ensure some synergy through sharing of experiences. Thoughtful arrangement of the seating ensures that people meet others with whom they do not normally work and helps with team building. We moved them to new seat places each day, determined by that day's activities.

Be careful not to treat them like a herd, with one person no better or different from the rest. Label their workbook and place tent cards before them (**printed** not written on both walls) with their name in large letters. If the participant is normally called Joe, write that, not Joseph.

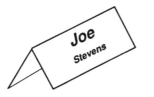

If the tent card looks good, they are impressed and the tide comes in. If you spelled their name wrong, the tide goes out.

But take care! Tom and Jerry sat next to each other because we considered them complementary. The tide should have come in but unfortunately Tom was dating Jerry's wife and he knew it!

Message. When arranging the seating, do not just think about personalities and job functions. They are people, so talk to their supervisors about your teaching plans. Make sure the tent card data is correct. Small mistakes count a great deal. Correct them **immediately.** Do not pretend that it does not matter just because it is easier to take that view.

Visual Aids

The workshop presentations were made as visual as possible using mainly overhead projector transparencies. If there is too much information on a slide, the text can be too small to be seen from the back of the room.

> # *A* Most Important Message
>
> Our Total Quality
>
> Process has been so
>
> successful that your pay
>
> from next month has been increased by
>
> 50%

Use the visual aids to drive them towards their workshop manual. Since the slides will be in the manual, occasionally refer them to the appropriate page. Familiarity with the manual is an effective way of persuading them to read about the quality process when they return to their workplace.

Message. Use minimum 25pt text size. If the text will not fit on one slide, don't make it smaller, but split the text between two slides. Make sure you have a large projection screen and the same goes for the TV monitor. **Good information** is essential, but make sure that **people can read it from the back of the room.**

4 **Group Dynamics**

There is nothing worse than sitting down for three days, never being asked a question and no requirement to do anything. A two hour lecture is hard to get through. String ten of them together over three days and you have an excellent formula for boredom where people do not learn much.

It is better to organise a dynamic atmosphere with lots of questions, group exercises and group participation. Have some fun! Encourage team spirit not only in the group exercises but also among the facilitators. This takes some time. Avoid like the plague changing a facilitator part way through a workshop. Their hostility after two days of team building has to be seen to be believed!

Workshops are often organised to contain a plenary session with a top management visitor giving a talk about his views on the quality process. Script him well, ensure he is consistent with everything else you are saying, his slides have the same format and he is a part of the team. Otherwise, his talk can sound good to him but he can damage the team-spirit of the workshop and at worst the participants feel hostile towards him and have no idea of the relevance of what he is saying.

If the participants have a role play exercise, give them some baseball hats with the role name on the front and paper hair around one for a lady. We always made sure that the character 'Sally Peters' was a man with a sense of humour and persuaded one of the ladies to put some lipstick on him.

Message. If you want them to learn about team building, then organise the workshops that way with group exercises. Ask questions and ensure a change of atmosphere at least every 20 minutes. There is no such thing as a wrong answer to a trainer's question; do not argue with the participants. Congratulate and thank them frequently for their input. Make them feel comfortable by showing them that they will forget much of the details of what they are learning. We had several slides called **comfort** slides, one of which was called **Walk-the-Talk**.

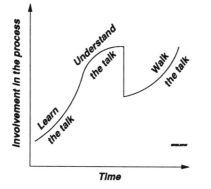

This slide ensures that they are aware that no one expects them to remember everything which is being taught. They need practice and a willingness to use their workshop manual as an operational reference book.

5   Trainer Sensitivity

The participants will have different attitudes towards the material you are teaching. Many of those who feel some hostility to this new process are doing a fine job already. Be sensitive to these issues and find out what they think. We asked all participants at the end of each workshop to fill in a workshop evaluation form. The analysis of these forms helped us change many details of the workshops to produce a better result. Make no mistake, it will probably be the details which make or break your Quality Process.

Message. Listen carefully, try not to argue with them and spend a few minutes at the end of each workshop analysing the workshop evaluation forms for workshop improvement ideas.

6   Trainer Enthusiasm

The enthusiasm and sincerity of the trainers is an essential requirement. Some of the participants came reluctantly and if the trainers seem uncommitted, the participants will detect it, and have him by the throat.

As trainer confidence rises so will their enthusiasm and the combination produces sincerity, a characteristic infinitely more important than being word perfect with the material. These characteristics will carry along a great many of the reluctant participants, who, in their own estimation, had something better to do that day.

When they return to the office and tell other people who have not yet been on the course that it is worthless, boring and so forth, the next group who arrive start further back than the ones you just taught.

Message.   Select the trainers carefully. They should be people of standing in the organisation. Good speakers who are poorly regarded by the workforce should be avoided. Give the trainers time to learn their material. Arrange for them to have training in presentation techniques and the opportunity to talk to each other to get some practice sessions and build facilitator teams.

7   Honesty

Honesty and sensitivity are very important. If you are asked a question and do not know the answer, say so. When someone asks a question, they do it because they either wanted an answer or were trying to make a point.

Message.   Find the answer and communicate it quickly to the person who asked. He probably did not expect the answer but may be impressed by your prompt and personal reply. Either way, you scored some points with that person by taking the trouble to find the answer quickly.

8   Humour

Which ever model you use for your quality process, they all tend to be a bit dry, so inject a little humour. If the trainers are enthusiastic and sincere but are too intense, they sound like soap-box evangelists. Try a slide like this:

> # Be thankful for problems,
> ## if they were less difficult, someone else with less ability might have your job.

Message.   Give them something to smile about, but resist the temptation to make fun of the quality process or the basic messages you are trying to convey. Create a fun atmosphere for at least some of the time.

⑨   **Be Organised**

Total Quality Management is about empowerment of people. You teach, coach and inform and then encourage them to take proper initiatives. When they want to do something differently, you cannot then say 'No, no ,no, you can't do that without approval in quintuplicate'.

Show them that you have an organisation which is effective and that you have planned for the future. Make them aware that the quality process gives them the power to get things done and that the organisation and logistics are in place to ensure that they get their own way when they are **right.**

Message.   Get the company organised before you release the flood gates of commitment to improvement. Total Quality is about managing the change you induce by empowering the people to take initiatives. You have to be ready to respond with a suitable unconstipated organisation structure.

5. FINAL MESSAGE

The need for an appropriate, well thought out Quality Process is, of course, essential. But many a good battle plan has been ruined by poor execution. The secret is to pay attention to detail. Treat everyone as individuals, try to do it right first time, be patient and eventually reap the rewards, first for the customers, then for the employees and finally for the shareholders, who will be delighted with your results.

Application of the Total Quality Management Process in the Manufacture of Polymers

S. H. Coulson

EXXON CHEMICAL INTERNATIONAL MARKETING, CADLAND ROAD, HYTHE,
SOUTHAMPTON SO4 6NP, UK

1 A MODEL FOR TOTAL QUALITY MANAGEMENT

A simple model (Figure 1) has been developed for the
Polymers Group of Exxon Chemical to show the basic
elements of Total Quality Management (TQM). This simple
model has been widely accepted and used for several years
throughout the Polymers Group. Let us consider the three
basic elements of the model –

Management Leadership

The process of TQM must be led by top management if it is
to succeed. The fourteen points for management stated by
Deming[1] are an excellent guide, but some
interpretation may be needed. The leadership challenge
is for management to develop an environment in which to
make continuous improvement, usually in many small steps.
The improvements will be by the elimination of waste and
the improvement in customer satisfaction – i.e.,
improvements in quality and productivity.

Quality System

The quality system documents the working rules of the
organisation[2]. It should spell out what has to be done,
when, where and by whom. The Polymers Group of Exxon
Chemical have obtained accreditation to ISO 9002 for all
their manufacturing sites. Note that ISO 9000 is not a
standard for TQM, it is only one of the many milestones
on the way. A most important aspect of the ISO 9000
system is the possibility for interaction between it and
the other elements of Management Leadership and Quality
Tools to give synergistic effects, if properly managed.

Quality Tools

Quality Tools range from the Seven Basic Tools (Figure 2)
through Data Analysis, Design of Experiments, and Process
Modelling to Process Automation. The use of tools and
techniques such as Competitive Benchmarking, Quality
Function Deployment, Total Productive Maintenance, Just
in Time should also be considered.

Other tools such as Auditing and Quality Economics are
also very important.
The author believes very strongly that, as a minimum, the
Seven Tools[3] must be understood and used by everyone in
the organisation.
The interaction with ISO 9000 can be very important here,
with for example, an ISO 9000 procedure to control an
application of SPC.(Statistical Process Control)

It takes a long time to get the basic elements of this
model in place and working. Therefore a number of topics
have been worked in parallel before moving on to TQM for
Improvement. Some of these activities are discussed
below.

2 TQM & `CUSTOMER INTERFACES´

Everyone is now familiar with the basic supply chain, but
typical supply chains are much more complex (Figure 3)
and the very difficult aspects of internal suppliers and
customers can be addressed. ISO 9000 can be used here to
help definition of such interfaces.
In our industry meeting the specification is a basic
fact, our customers are interested in how well we meet
the specification. This philosophy is not addressed in
ISO 9000, but can be addressed through SPC and
statistical characterisation of processes (Process
Capability Indices) and through the Taguchi Loss
Function[4]. Coulson and Cousans have described the
process of supplier and customer joint improvement
programmes[5] and have highlighted key customer
requirements (Figure 4). In Exxon Chemical we have tried
to follow a very basic concept formulated by Deming
"Supplier and Customer Working Together for their Mutual
Benefit." The results are depicted in Figure 5.

3 TQM & `MEASUREMENT´

The simple equation of variance has been a key tool for
improvement in working with polymers. The Standard
Deviation (STD) of a Product comprises variability
from both the manufacturing and the measurement
processes, such that -

$$(STD)^2 Product = (STD)^2 Process + (STD)^2 Test \qquad [1]$$

Our first SPC applications were in the laboratory[6] where
we were able to define test capabilities and test STDs.
The dramatic effects of reducing test variability in
reducing the measured Product STD and hence apparent
process capability, without touching the manufacturing
process, are shown in Figure 6. This understanding is of
great importance in an industry where many of the tests
are empirical, and often have high variability.

4 TQM & `PROCESS CONTROL´

A key component of TQM is in progressing from traditional
`Quality Control´ on the PRODUCT (Figure 7) to
`Statistical Process Control´ on the PROCESS (Figure 8).
The first step is to define the process, and here Flow
Charting[3] is an essential tool. ISO 9004 philosophy can
be used[7] in a process survey to further define what
happens. There is great deal of information about the
statistics of control charting and SPC, but very little
on what you should DO with the charts. Ford have some
pointers in their Ford Q101 System[8], but we have found
that the most important part of control charting is the
management of the actions resulting from charting. This
is an area where the interaction between ISO 9000 and SPC
is critical, and we have developed ISO 9000 type
procedures to manage SPC applications, Figure 9.
If this approach is not taken, SPC will only result in
fossilisation of processes, in a state of control, with
predictable and consistent performance run to run, year
to year - with no improvement.

5 TQM & `DATA ANALYSIS´

The approaches used in much of industry for data analysis
are quite revealing. The traditional `Eyeball´ approach
is much used still, and, in fact, the increased use of
computers and the associated heaps of printouts appear
to have encouraged the `Eyeball´ technique. Computers
have also facilitated the use of very powerful
mathematical/statistical data analysis techniques. The
results of such analyses are often presented in ways
which can be difficult to understand and often are
difficult to relate in a practical way to the underlying
processes. Julian[8] made a plea for computers to be used
in the graphical mode only - "graphs rule, OK?".
We have treated data analysis as a process, and have
applied the TQM philosophy to it. Where a complex data
analysis process has been used, the process has been
shown as a flow chart to aid understanding. This
approach to data analysis has been developed further in
the rules for improvement teams at ECL Butyl Polymers, at
Fawley, UK, where people are expected to come to meetings
with -
        Facts, not opinions
        Pictures, not lists of numbers
        Preliminary data analysis
In this way meetings are effective, actions can be easily
and clearly defined, and, the meetings are short.
Another important question is "Is the right tool being
used?" In many process industries a subtle cause of
variability is step changes in the mean, as shown in
Figure 10, where there is step change of one standard
deviation. Can you see where the change occurred? The
Shewhart Chart is not very efficient in detecting such
changes, and cannot be used to determine EXACTLY when the

change occurred. However, if the CUSUM chart is used as
a historical diagnostic tool[3], the point of change can be
determined precisely, as shown in Figure 11. Then ISO
9000 and the traceability system have to be invoked, to
determine what happened here - say a catalyst change, new
supplier etc. This change is an Assignable Cause, and
must be eliminated before SPC can be used properly.

6 TQM & `IMPROVEMENT´

When the stages detailed above had been worked through it
became time to tackle improvement. This was particularly
important after the ISO 9002 accreditation and the
introduction of SPC. ISO 9002 and SPC introductions often
give a stagnation period and, in fact, after an initial
once-off improvement, do not give further improvement.
In fact no further improvement will be obtained without
management activity to plan and to lead improvement,
Figure 12. Improvement will not simply happen,
improvement must be planned and managed, Figure 13. The
effective route to improvement is through improvement
teams, where peoples´ knowledge is tapped and used. This
process also needs careful management, Figure 14.

7 TQM & `BENEFITS´

The first benefits to be seen should be `Internal´ to
include a number of key items.
The management style should have changed from
`Firefighting and shouting´ to `planning and leading´
which will result in attitude changes from `Them `n´ us´
to `Us `n´ us´. This will be seen as a `buzz´ about the
place, with everyone being enthusiastic and involved.
The tangible results will be improvements in quality and
productivity, thence reductions in costs.
The `External´ benefits to be gained are shown in Figure
16. The use of TQM for improvement results in better
products and services, at lower costs, which can be
exploited to give higher profitability.

8 REFERENCES

1. W.E. Deming, 'Quality, Productivity and Competitive Position', MIT, Cambridge, USA, 1982
2. J.G.Pimblott (Ed.), 'Profit & Growth Through Quality', Plastics & Rubber Institute, London, 1988.
3. S.H.Coulson (Ed.),'Managing Improvement - Where to Start, Plastics & Rubber Institute, London, 1989.
4. S.H.Coulson & J.A.Cousans, 'Quality Today in Polymer Processing, RAPRA, Pergammon Press, Oxford, 1991.
5. S.H.Coulson & J.A.Cousans, 'Making Quality Improvement Happen' in 'Total Quality Management' J.M.Buist & S.H.Coulson (Eds), Plastics & Rubber Institute, London, 1990
6 S.H.Coulson & J.A.Cousans, 'SPC - its Role within the Synthetic Rubber Industry, <u>Plastics & Rubber International.</u> August, 1986.
7. S.H.Coulson & J.A.Cousans, 'Beyond SPC - a Case Study' <u>Quality Forum.</u> Vol 16, No.4, p174, December 1990.
8. Anon., 'Q.101 Quality System Standard', Ford Motor Company, 1990.
9. K.Julien, Statisticians - Keep it Simple', <u>QA News.</u> Vol.15, No.7, July 1989.

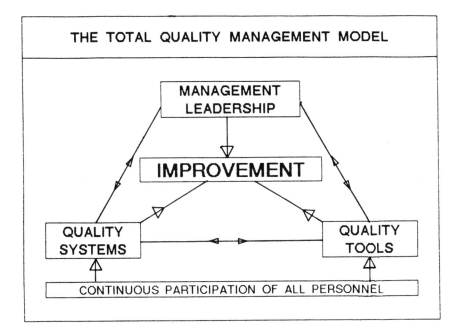

Figure 1.   The Exxon Chemical Total Quality Model

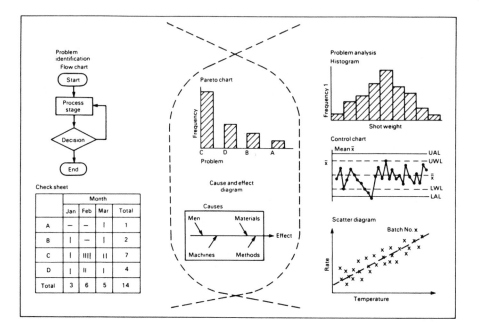

Figure 2. The Seven Tools of Improvement

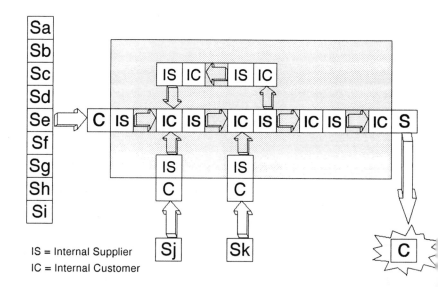

IS = Internal Supplier
IC = Internal Customer

Figure 3. A Typical Supply Chain in the Chemical Industry

	CAPABILITY ABILITY TO MEET SPECIFICATION WITHOUT SELECTION (CpK ≥ 2)	
CONSISTENCY BATCH to BATCH DELIVERY to DELIVERY PLANT to PLANT	CENTERING ABILITY ON TARGET MID-SPEC (CpK ≥ 2)	CONVERGENCY SPREAD OF RESULTS REDUCING TO TARGET (CpK ≥ 2)
	CREDIBILITY PROVISION OF VALID & USEFUL STATISTICAL ANALYSES	

Figure   4.   Customer Perception of Today´s Supplier

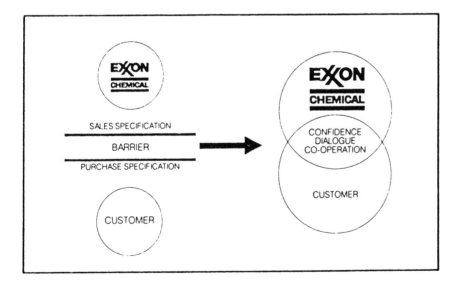

Figure   5.   Old & New Customer/Supplier Relationships

PROCESS VARIANCE	TEST VARIANCE	SUM. TEST & PROCESS VARIANCES	PRODUCT STANDARD DEVIATION	PRODUCT CAPABILITY INDEX (Cp)
1.21	1.21	2.42	1.56	1.07
1.21	0.36	1.57	1.25	1.33
1.21	0.04	1.25	1.12	1.49

PRODUCT STANDARD DEVIATION (STD)
= SQUARE ROOT of SUM OF VARIANCES

PRODUCT CAPABILITY INDEX =
SPEC. RANGE / 6xPRODUCT STD.
AND, SPECIFICATION RANGE = 10

Figure 6. Test Variability & Capability Improvement

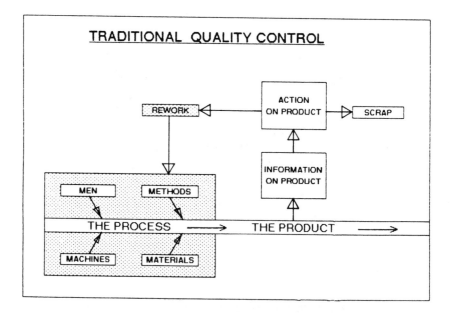

Figure 7. Traditional Quality Control

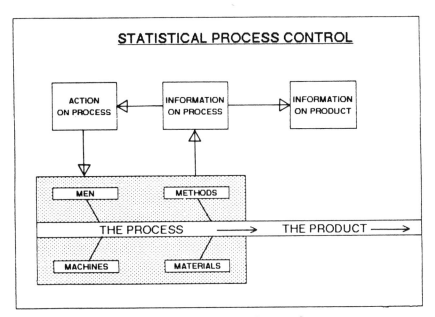

Figure 8. Statistical Process Control

A PROCEDURE FOR MANAGING SPC

1 DEFINE SELECTION OF PARAMETERS FOR SPC APPLICATION

2 USE THE EQUATION OF VARIANCE TO DETERMINE IF THE MEASURED VARIABILITY IS FROM THE PROCESS OR TEST.

3 DISCUSS WITH OPERATORS HOW THEY CONTROL NOW

4 SELECT APPROPRIATE CHARTING TECHNIQUE

5 DEFINE STATISTICAL RULES FOR 'OUT-OF-CONTROL'

6 DEFINE AND AGREE ACTIONS TO BE TAKEN WHEN IN 'OUT-OF-CONTROL' SITUATIONS

7 RECORD CAUSES OF 'OUT-OF-CONTROL'

8 ANALYSE CAUSES OF 'OUT-OF-CONTROL'

9 TAKE ACTIONS TO REMOVE CAUSES OF 'OUT-OF-CONTROL'

10 RECALCULATE CONTROL LIMITS, AND, GO BACK TO STEP 2 ABOVE

Figure 9. A Procedure for Managing SPC

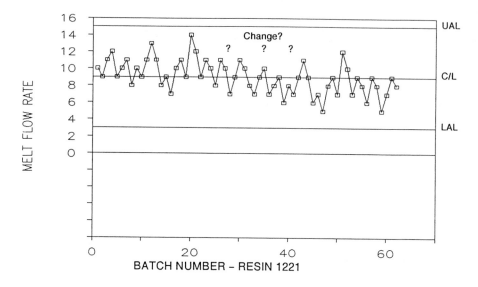

Figure 10. Shewhart Chart and a Step Change

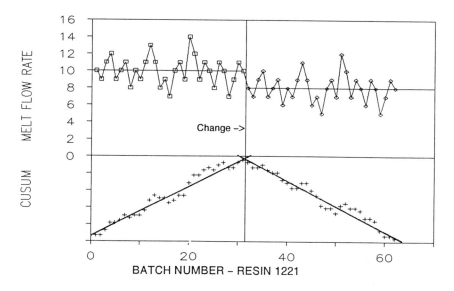

Figure 11. Shewhart Chart, CUSUM and a Step Change

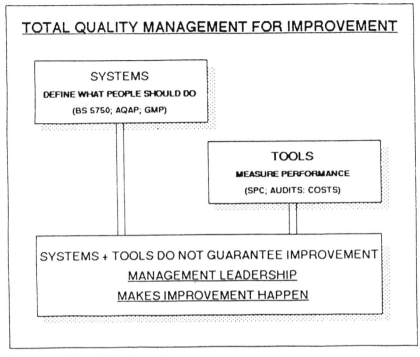

Figure 12.   TQM for Improvement

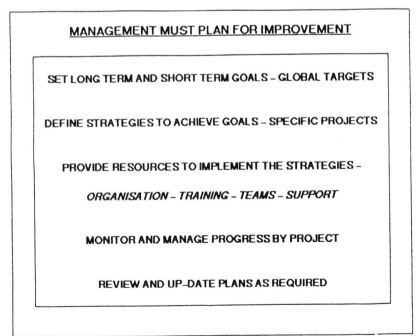

Figure 13.   Planning for Improvement

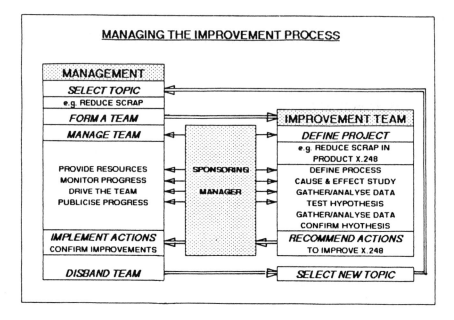

Figure 14.   Management & Improvement   Teams

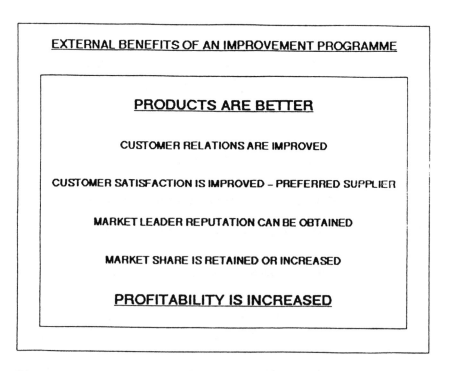

Figure 15.   External Benefits of TQM

Mother Nature: A Quality Supplier?

D. Howling

CERESTAR UK LTD., TRAFFORD PARK, MANCHESTER M17 1PA, UK

Total quality has, as its name suggests, many facets and this symposium is an illustration of this. One of these facets which is of major importance is the relationship between customer and supplier, internal and external; a mutual understanding of needs and expectations.

Quality systems like ISO 9002 prescribe methods for the consistent achievement of quality standards by documenting procedures, process parameters and specifications.

All this assumes that the supplier is able to influence his own process completely and that the ultimate supplier is available for discussion and dialogue. Where that ultimate supplier is nature itself and the supplier chain is the amorphous ill defined and not well controlled agricultural system that gives problems.

These problems are not insuperable in my view and I have had involvement with a number of cases in Europe though they do need special approaches and the purpose of this paper is to illustrate these by way of a case study.

This case took place in the years 1983/1985, when for agropolitical and economic reasons the source of Zea mays-maize to the European starch industry was changed from N.America, where it had been grown for wet milling since the process was patented by William Polson of Brown and Polson fame in 1840, to France. This itself was a non quality decision as it was taken almost unilaterally with little time for planning the change.

Now the French grow a lot of maize but they had never supplied it
to the wet milling industry, they had used it as an animal
feedstuff for force feeding to geese to produce pate de foie gras
and like delicacies. As customers the geese and the wet milling
industry had different expectations and needs. The latter had to
produce high quality starch in good economic yield from the maize
for chemical and biochemical conversion to products used in a
wide variety of industries from food, through fermentation,
pharmaceutical to papermaking and adhesive preparations.

Before we can proceed meaningfully I must describe briefly what
maize is and the wet milling process by which the starch is
separated from it. Figure I shows the typical composition of
maize. Figure II shows the wet milling process steps.

Germ separation by hydrocyclones is the first stage but the two
key separations so far as our discussions are concerned are the
separation of the starch and protein from the fibre by filtration
on wedge wire screens after impact milling and the
separation of starch and protein (gluten) by centrifugation i.e.
the separation of the endosperm fractions.

Figure III shows the comparison of the two locations from the
point of view of the major considerations for wet milling
quality. It can be seen from this that the two sources of supply
were very different in almost all respects. It is not surprising
that the initial performance of French corn was poor giving
yields at both the fibre separation and protein separation stage.
This gave a number of disadvantages not only of economics but of
meeting the specification for our finished products and hence
fulfilling our customers expectations.

Taking the T.Q.M. approach to the problem was addressed by
working with the supplier to resolve the problem in the various
areas as follows.

Climate

This is really where mother nature is at her most capricious.
There have been some attempts to influence weather but as we meet
here in Manchester the folly of this approach is evident.

The problem here is that for good separation of the endosperm
fractions a certain 'ripeness' of the maize is required. This
depends upon the variety of maize sown. It goes almost without
saying that on the prairies of the mid-west, sufficient sun is
guaranteed for the varieties sown but this had evolved
empirically without study of the real needs of the wet milling
process.

FRACTION		STARCH	PROTEINS
Nature	Proportion	(%)	(%)
Whole grain	100	71.5	10.3
Endosperm	82.5	86.4	9.5
Germ	11.5	8.2	18.8
Bran etc.	6.0	4.0	3.7

FIGURE I   TYPICAL COMPOSITION OF COMMERCIAL MAIZE

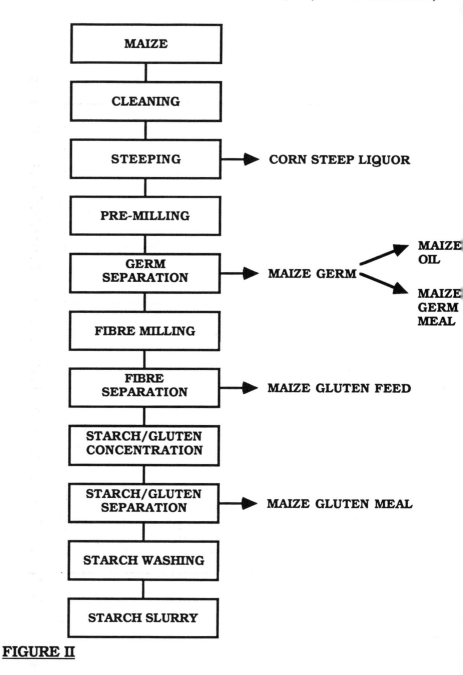

FIGURE II

BLOCK DIAGRAM OF THE MAIZE WET-MILLING PROCESS

	U.S.	FRENCH (1983)
CLIMATE	HIGH SUN	MARGINAL SUN
VARIETY	DENT.	VARIOUS
AGRICULTURAL PRACTICE	LARGE PRAIRIES	SMALL FIELDS
MOISTURE ON HARVEST (%)	25-30	25-42
DRYING PROCESS	CONTROLLED LOW TEMPERATURE	VARIOUS

FIGURE III   IMPORTANT PARAMETERS FOR GRAIN QUALITY

In France it was different, sunlight is marginal, comparisons of 1983 a good year and 1984 a bad year show that. Thus knowledge of the climate history of a crop is important and we have developed mathematical models based on daily reports from 35 weather stations in the regions of France so that at harvest we could know the climate history of the area and select accordingly. This assumes the supplier can keep supplies segregated.

The other effect of the climate more specifically concerns the temperature and hence residual moisture of the corn at harvest. The lower the moisture the less artificial drying is necessary which is beneficial to millability.

Variety

Some varieties even after receiving adequate sunlight mill better than others and dent corn is the preferred variety. More important however is that the kernels are of uniform size as the first degermination milling relies on the clearance between teeth in a mill being just sufficient to crack open the maize. Small beans passing through are no good but over milling causes breakdown of the fibre fractions and makes separation more difficult. The problem here is the large number of varieties which were sown and the tendency to use high yielding hybrid varieties which gave good feed values but which were poor for wet milling. This practice had been encouraged by authorities in the quest to make the EEC self sufficient in cereals. The need for the wet milling industry was to encourage the farmers to plant suitable varieties of similar kernel size.

Agricultural Practice

This really follows on from the question of variety discussed above. To obtain good millability then uniformly sized kernels of known good milling variety have to be obtained. With large prairies this was easily done but in France maize is collected and dried by co-operatives. One such co-operative producing 400,000 t.a. maize was supplied by 7000 farmers. Each farmer had complete control over which variety he planted and when he harvested it. So far as field size was concerned these could be minute - even odd corners of fields of other crops and in one village the traffic island had been planted with corn. This clearly led to a very hetrogenous crop in a given silo. Bearing in mind the needs of our process a far from ideal situation.

What the wet milling industry did was draw up a code of practice for the growers outlining the needs of the wet milling industry in these areas. It has to be said that incentives may have to be given to the grain producer to adopt these practices.

1. DAMAGE (HEAT AND MOULD)

2. KERNAL WEIGHT

3. SIZE VARIATION

4. STEEP INDEX

5. SEDIMENTATION

6. PILOT PLANT

PREDICTIVE TESTS

FIGURE IV

1   KNOW WHAT IS IMPORTANT TO <u>YOUR</u> PROCESS.

2   MAKE SUPPLIER AWARE OF THOSE NEEDS.

3.   STUDY THE FACTORS WHICH AFFECT THOSE NEEDS.

4.   WORK WITH SUPPLIER ON A PROCEDURE TO ASSURE SUITABILITY.

5.   MONITOR CONDITIONS OUTSIDE HUMAN CONTROL IN THE FIELD.

6.   DEVISE DIAGNOSTIC TEST FOR SUITABILITY AND SPECIFY.

7.   BE VIGILANTLY AND FLEXIBLE IN SOURCING.

FIGURE V   T.Q.M. - FOR NATURAL RAW MATERIALS

Drying

Corn as harvested in the field has a moisture higher than the
15-17% of stable maize for storage. This reduction in moisture
has to be achieved through artificial drying. How this is done
is crucial to yield of starch.

In France again the number of these and the method of operation
varied considerably. Over 3000 existed in 1983 of 5 major types.
Due to energy economics and throughput considerations the tendency
had been to use high temperatures. Starch is separated from the
protein by centrifugation of the higher density granules from the
gluten fraction. Above $60^{\circ}C$ starch granules begin to swell
taking in moisture as they do and this reduced the density of the
granule. It is obvious that heating above $60^{\circ}C$ progressively
reduces the efficiency of the separation.

There is a need for a progressive replacement of the driers and a
code of practice for drying maize for wet milling was drawn up
and encouragement was given to the co-operatives to begin a
programme to replace existing unsuitable driers with low
temperature two pass driers and other designs which met the code
of practice.

Predictive Tests

One of the needs at the beginning of this exercise was for a test
which could predict the milling performance of maize to correlate
known sources of grain with performance. In the research phase
long complicated tests could be used - even pilot plant studies.
However, as the process became more refined then a test which
could be defined in a specification and was simple enough to be
performed in the field by the supplier was needed. Those studied
are shown in Figure IV. Damage is the easiest and sedimentation
which takes 24 hours but is very reliable have been devised and
are regularly used.

Conclusion

I have illustrated the dilemmas which faced the starch industry
in 1983 - on the surface the conditions of maize supply from
France could not have been less suited to our needs but today
through the total involvement of supplier and customer working
together a suitable supply has been established.

From this experience I have listed in Figure V a number of stages
which are necessary in a total quality process, after which I am
sure it is possible to consider that mother nature is a total
quality supplier.

ISO 9000 an International Building Block for or Barrier to Total Quality Management

B. G. Henshaw

INTERNATIONAL BIOSYNTHETICS LTD., HALEBANK, WIDNES, CHESHIRE WA8 8NS, UK

INTRODUCTION

The need for an international standard for Quality Systems had been recognised by the International Standards Organisation in the 1970's when quality was emerging as a new or rather rediscovered force in commerce and industry. In 1979 ISO formed Technical Committee 176 to look at the establishment of international standards for Quality. This committee surveyed what was available in the world as models for an international standard for Quality Systems.

Two of the most developed standards for Quality Systems at that time were those of Canada and the United Kingdom. BS 5750 had first been published in 1979 as a development from a range of military and civil standards. It is arguable that the UK was the world leader in Quality system standards, and indeed that this remains the case. Eventually the British Standard BS 5750 (1979) was chosen as the model and ISO 9000 (1987) series was issued. In the UK this was dual numbered with BS 5750 (1987) and is hence identical.

Many other countries adopted this standard as their own national standard and it was translated into a number of languages without modification. For example, in the American standard ANSI/ASQC 90 - 94,[1] the only substantial changes are the use of transatlantic English, e.g. the spelling of "colour" would be changed to color. The matrix attached as Figure 1 shows the international position in 1989/90 when as a group IBIS was seeking registration of sites in the USA and Belgium to ISO 9002 and also seeking to upgrade an ISO 9002 registration in the UK to ISO 9001.

The Hardware Nature of the Standard

The 1987 version of the ISO 9000 standard is written in

QUALITY SYSTEMS STANDARDS MATRIX					
STANDARDS BODY	LEVEL 1	LEVEL 2	LEVEL 3	GUIDELINES	
ISO	ISO 9001: 1987	ISO 9002: 1987	ISO 9003: 1987	ISO 9000 : 1987	ISO 9004: 1987
UNITED STATES	ANSI/ASQC Q91-1987	ANSI/ASQC Q92-1987	ANSI/ASQC Q93-1987	ANSI/ASQC Q90-1987	ANSI/ASQC Q94-1987
CEN	EN 29001	EN 29002	EN 29003	EN 29000	EN 29004
BELGIUM	NBN X 50-003	NBN X 50-004	NBN X 50-005	NBN X 50-002	-
CANADA	CSA Z299.1-85	CSA Z299.2-85	CSA Z299.4-85	CSA Z299.0-86	CSA Q420-87
FRANCE	NF X 50-131	NF X 50-132	NF X 50-133	NF X 50-121	NF X 50-122
NETHERLANDS	NEN 2646	NEN 2647	NEN 2648	NPR 2645	NPR 2650
NORWAY	NS 5801	NS 5802	NS 5803	-	-
SWITZERLAND	SN 029 100A	SN 029 100B	SN 029 100C	-	-
UNITED KINGDOM	BS 5750: Part 1 (ISO 9001 - 1987)	BS 5750: Part 2 (ISO 9002 - 1987)	BS 5750: Part 3 (ISO 9003 - 1987)	BS 5750: Part 0 Sec 0.1 (ISO 9000 - 1987)	BS 5750: Part 0 Sec 0.2 (ISO 9004 - 1987)
WEST GERMANY	DIN ISO 9001	DIN ISO 9002	DIN ISO 9003	DIN ISO 9000	DIN ISO 9004

FIGURE 1

largely hardware terms, that is in the language of
hardware industry where products consist of
manufactured pieces, parts or assemblies thereof. This
makes interpretation by process industry, service and
software providers difficult. As a consequence there
has been a proliferation of notes interpreting the
meaning of the standard and how it applies in different
industries. These notes provide a translation of the
standard into the language and applications of each
industry, but even with these guidance notes the
service of an outside consultant or an experienced user
of the standard in the specific industry is generally
necessary for companies seeking registration to the
standard. ISO in their "Vision 2000"[2] have expressed
the desire to remove this necessity for additional
application specific guidance notes, but this has had
little effect at the present time. For the chemical
process industries the most useful guidance note to
interpretation of the standard is the CEFIC guidelines
to EN29000, available through the CIA[3].

Experience in Gaining ISO Registrations Outside the UK

IBIS had considered as a group how we would go about
securing registration on our sites. BSI would, of
course, carry out assessments in all parts of the world
but there are a number of disadvantages in using this
approach. Firstly, the travel costs involved for our
USA site would have been prohibitive. Secondly in our
Belgian site the language would be a problem with BSI
having to take along an interpreter to be able to
understand the working documents. Although the senior
management all spoke English, the language of the shop
floor was Flemish and the instructions which the
operators used to carry out their manufacturing
operations were all written in that language. We would
have needed to provide a Quality Manual two in languages
with considerable risk of additional complexity and
confusion. In addition, it was felt that a local
registration to the national standard of the country in
which each site was located would lead to far more
identification with the standard by the employees of
the local companies.

For these reasons we decided to pursue a local
registration to the national standard of the country in
which each site was located. There were, however, some
considerable problems with local registration to the
standard ; the main problem with the local
registration approach was the shortage of accredited
organisations to do the assessment. In the USA it
proved impossible to get accreditation by a US based
agency but we were able to have assessment carried
out by the Canadian Standards organisation. This led to
our first surprise when we found that the Canadian
standard[4] was not word identical with ISO 9002 but
actually was quite different with so called equivalent

levels to the ISO 9000 series; the Canadian standard has 4 levels, sorting, verifying, reacting and preventing which are akin to charting progress in Quality understanding. However, we were able to secure registration for our US sites by the end of 1989 to an ISO 9003 Z299.4 combined registration.

This may seem very curious to the people in the U.K. who are familiar with ISO 9003, and know that it is normally used for non-manufacturing organisations but that is the way the registration was carried out by the Canadian Standards Authority; one consequence of this registration is that internal audits are not a mandatory part of our registration in the USA.

In Belgium the problem proved even more intractable and despite early negotiations with some local accreditation agencies we were quite unable to make progress and had to choose BSI to carry out the registration.

The Benefits and Costs of ISO 9000 Registration

There were several benefits which we found on gaining registration. We had planned to have a documented systems base for quality improvement and that is precisely what we got with a very well documented and controlled procedurally based system. The improvements brought about by having gained an ISO 9002 registration in the UK led to the decision to extend our registration to ISO 9001; this 9001 registration took in our research and development activities. This area has benefited greatly from registration with a clear understanding now among all of our technologists of how new products are progressed from enquiry through to production. It has helped to break down the traditional "brick over the wall" approach to development by fostering effective communication.

Other major benefits have been a reduction in the rejection rate for company products by about half, probably due to the corrective action requirement; this requirement for corrective action is one of the strongest elements of the standard if used correctly and can form a very firm base for process improvement. Training is also addressed and the training records within IBIS have improved enormously since registration. We also have made some considerable savings in our scrap and rework rates since introduction of the standard.

In terms of costs for a site of 350 in the UK we incurred consultancy fees of about 10,000 pounds for our 9002 registration plus I would estimate 4 or 5 man years of procedural effort spread evenly over the company through most departments. There is an on-going cost of registration payable to BSI of about

3000 pounds per annum and maintenance and update of
procedures requires 1 - 2 people full time. Update to
part 1 probably cost a further 3-4,000 pounds plus 1-2
man years.

ISO 9000 and Total Quality Management

How does ISO 9000 relate to the activities necessary to
implement a Total Quality Management Programme? Well,
first of all it is not designed as a TQM standard,
although Section 0 does give some useful guidance. Both
BSI and ISO are now working on Total Quality Management
standards. BSI are working on a new draft standard
which is currently out for comment which will provide
new parts for BS 4891, this is going through Technical
Committee QMS 22. ISO is working on a new series of
standards, its 10,000 series, which will cover Total
Quality Management.

Figure 2 shows the clauses of both ISO 9000 and the
new draft British Standard for Total Quality
Management, and some considerable differences can be
seen.One major difference between ISO 9000 and any TQM
process is that there is little in the way of a
philosophical base in the ISO 9000 series; this is
perhaps not surprising for an auditable series of
standards which form the basis for contractual
negotiations and obligations. The lack of a
philosophical base means it is relatively easy for the
senior management team within a company to provide some
resource to gain an ISO registration and delegate the
whole process and all the activities involved with it
to others.

TQM on the other hand, requires leadership, commitment
and, yes, activity from the senior management team of a
company. A fundamental transformation of management
style is required, a move from a directive to a process
management style as described by Myron Tribus; this is
much more demanding and requires far more commitment
and understanding by the senior management team than
the "lets get a certificate" approach of ISO 9000
registration.

ISO 9000 concentrates very much on a control
philosophy, rather than requiring empowerment of
employees. The way the standard is interpreted by many
assessors is based on an underlying assumption that
unless an activity is documented, it hasn't been
carried out, with the requirement for "objective
evidence" of any actions. This can conflict with the
empowerment and personal initiative elements of a TQM
process.

The standard is not judgemental, and the assessors are
discouraged from making improvement suggestions. It is
possible to run processes in the most ludicrously

FIGURE 2.

<u>ISO 9001</u>   <u>DRAFT BRITISH STANDARD</u>
                                         <u>GUIDE TO TQM (BS 4891)</u>

                                         PART 1 MANAGEMENT

REQUIREMENTS   **SECTION 3. FUNDAMENTAL CONCEPTS**

Management Responsibility   1.   Commitment

Quality System   2.   Customer Satisfaction

Contract Review   3.   Quality Losses

Design Control   4.   Participation by All

Document Control   5.   Process Management

Purchasing   6.   Continuous Improvement

Purchaser Supplied Product   7.   Problem Identification

Product Identification   8.   Alignment of Corporate
and Traceability   Objectives and Individual
                                          Attitudes
Process Control
                                     9.   Personal Accountability
Inspection and Testing
                                    10.   Personal Development
Inspection, Measuring
and Test Equipment   **PART 2 QUALITY IMPROVEMENT**

Inspection and Test Status   SECTION 3. FUNDAMENTAL CONCEPTS

Control of Non Conforming   SECTION 4. MANAGING FOR
Products   QUALITY IMPROVEMENT

Corrective Action   SECTION 5. A METHODOLOGY FOR
                                                QUALITY IMPROVEMENT
Handling Storage, Packaging
and Delivery   SECTION 6. SUPPORTING TOOLS
                                                AND TECHNIQUES
Quality Records

Internal Quality Audits

Training

Servicing

Statistical Techniques

inefficient manner, have very high reject rates, and many customer complaints but provided this is well documented this will not affect a company's registration. This, of course, is quite the opposite of TQM processes, where constant improvement of product and process is a pre-requisite. As a nation can the U.K. afford to take this approach?

One of ISO 9000's greatest strengths is also one of its weaknesses. "Quality Assurance is not a paper generator" is an adage of many Quality Consultants, but in our experience each BSI 5750/ISO 9000 audit leads to generation of more paperwork. Documentation of processes is forced by the standard and this is essential for improvement purposes, as it is difficult to improve a process before it has been written down. Control of process changes is a key area within the chemical industry and the standard has certainly ensured that we have this control and that no un-authorised process changes are made. However, it seems that the paperwork which we are asked to generate often has no perceptible added value, which leads me to ask again "can we as a nation afford to continue in this way and is this bureaucratic approach within the spirit of the 9000 series?"

In summary then, ISO 9000 does not address several TQM fundamentals but it does have a great deal of strength in many areas; ISO 9000 registration gives a company a documented quality system with excellent document control and prevention of unauthorised changes. It gives a system base for improvement but can create non value added bureaucracy and prevent empowerment and personal initiative. One of the dangers in achieving an ISO 9000 registration is the feeling among senior management that having gained an ISO 9000 certificate they have "done" Quality and can now move onto something else. It is often viewed by senior managers as the end of the Quality process rather than the beginning.

ISO 9000 is not designed as a TQM standard, it does not lead automatically to management committment to Quality or to the adoption of TQM as a management philosophy and method. ISO 9000 can be used as a stepping stone and a system base for implementation of Total Quality Management; it will help companies to hold the gains from TQM programmes by documentation and regular audit. Other national standards and national awards are better suited to move companies forward from the base which it provides towards TQM.There are several awards which give elements of and measurements for TQM eg the Baldridge award or Deming award. Alternatively the new British Standard on Total Quality Management will serve this purpose.

REFERENCES

1. American National Standard, ANSI/ASQC Q90 to Q94 1987, American Society For Quality Control, 310 Wisconsin Avenue, Milwaukee, Wisconsin 53203, USA.
2. D. Marquardt, J. Chove, K.E. Jensen, K. Petrick, J. Pyle and D. Strahle, Vision 2000: The Strategy For The ISO 9000 Series Standards In The 90's, Quality Progress, May, 1991.
3. EN 29001, ISO 9001 Guidelines For Use By The Chemical Industry, CEFIC, Available From The Chemical Industries Association, Kings Buildings, Smiths Square, London SW1P 3JJ.
4. Canadian National Standard, Can3-Z299.4-85, Quality Assurance Program Category 4, Canadian Standards Association, 178 Rexdale Boulevard, Rexdale (Toronto), Ontario,Canada, M9W 1R3.

Toll Manufacturing and ISO 9002—Some Problems and Solutions

Norman Gee

BAXENDEN CHEMICALS LTD., PARAGON WORKS, BAXENDEN, ACCRINGTON, LANCASHIRE BB5 2SL, UK

1 INTRODUCTION

What I've been asked to talk to you about is Toll Manufacturing and ISO 9002 - some problems and solutions.

For those of you who aren't too familiar with Baxenden Chemicals, we're primarily polymer manufacturers, although we also manufacture some speciality organics, and we produce both 'own products' as well as Toll Manufacturing for other companies.

As the person within Baxenden who was mainly responsible for setting up the procedures to enable registration to ISO 9002 to be achieved (which, incidentally, we did in August 1989) I had to consider both the 'own products' and the Toll Manufacturing operations.

From that point of view I believe I was fortunate. Having an existing Toll Manufacturing operation meant that the procedures had to be written with that in mind - it might not have been as easy if we had tried to add Toll Manufacturing after registering soley for 'own products'.

Toll manufacturing appears to be one of the growth areas within the Chemical Sector even in, or perhaps because of, these recessional times. Many companies find that it is more cost effective to 'farm out' certain manufacturing operations to specialists, rather than install expensive manufacturing plant or facilities to handle unpleasant materials. This is particularly true in the early days of a new product, where initial volume does not justify capital investment.

As many companies seeking Toll Manufacturing services are themselves registered to ISO 9000, they are fully aware of their requirements for suppliers and subcontractors.

Assuming the manufacturer is also registered, unless he is experienced in Toll Manufacturing, he may be unaware of the detail difference between manufacturing an 'own product' range and manufacturing as a subcontractor.

Unless the quality system has been well thought out to take into account the needs of a Toll Manufacturing operation, there are many problems which can arise.

'Bolting on' a Toll Manufacturing operation to a system designed to cope with only 'own products' manufacturing will almost certainly lead to problems. Some of the most obvious points can be overlooked.

Most of the points I am going to make will perhaps be familiar to those with existing Toll Manufacturing operations, but perhaps not familiar to those intending to use Toll Manufacturing as a "capacity filler" or as an extension to an existing 'own product' range.

All the points are what I would describe as 'detail' points and highlight what has to be considered and the flexibility required within a quality system dealing with Toll Manufacturing.

2   SOME PROBLEMS AND SOLUTIONS

Let's start looking at some of the problems.

Problem 1.   Is the proposed Toll Manufacturing operation within the scope of registration?

The examples I'm about to give regarding scope are taken from the BSI BUYERS GUIDE.

It specifically mentions in the front of the Buyers Guide:-

"IT SHOULD BE NOTED THAT THE FIRMS MAY SUPPLY PRODUCTS OR SERVICES OUTSIDE THE SCOPE OF THEIR LICENCE/ REGISTRATION. PURCHASERS SHOULD THEREFORE BE AWARE THAT THE LICENCE/REGISTRATION RELATES ONLY TO THE PRODUCTS AND SERVICES LISTED ON THE COMPANY'S CERTIFICATE AND SUMMARISED IN THIS GUIDE"

For example, if the existing registration is:-

For "The manufacture and supply of chemicals containing sulphur"

and the proposed Toll Manufacturing operation is:-

For the manufacture of imidazole.

It is not difficult to see that the proposed operation

would not fall within the existing scope of registration
- imidazole is not a sulphur containing chemical.

Just because the Toll Manufacturing job isn't within
the scope of registration it doesn't of course mean that
the supplier is not capable of doing the job.

Solution

So when setting up an ISO 9002 system it is wise to
have as wide a scope as possible.

For example, a company both manufacturing speciality
organics in their own right and Toll Manufacturing a number
of products may have a scope of registration along the
lines

for   "The manufacture and supply of synthetic organic
        chemicals including Toll Manufacture"

The above scope is terrific - it doesn't limit the
manufacturer at all in the organic chemical field.

Problem 2. Do you have the necessary Plant and Test and
Measuring Equipment?

Whilst this would form part of an overall technical
feasibility evaluation before taking on a Toll Manufacturing job there is a requirement within ISO 9002 that a
formal evaluation take place.

In the case of Toll Manufacturing this could include:-

1.   That plant instruments are capable of measuring
process variables to the required accuracy and precision
- what may be satisfactory for 'own product' manufacture
may not be so for the Toll Manufacturing job in mind.

e.g. Temperature control requirements may be more
rigorous for the Toll Manufacturing job than for 'own
products' production.

2.   The same comment applies for QC instrumentation.

Solution

A thorough 'audit' of the plant and facilities appropriate to the Toll Manufacturing job is required.

It is worth bearing in mind that any manufacturing
or test equipment you intend to purchase for the Toll
Manufacturing job should, where possible, be identical to
that of the customer and that additional training or
skills may be required.

And remember also that the customer may already be making this material on his own plant - it could just be that he's short of capacity - in that case he'll know exactly what type of plant and equipment is required.

Problem 3. Have you Formal Agreement of Product and Process Specifications with the Customer?

In my view this is one of the most important points.

For 'own products' the specifications for a particular product is effectively agreed with a customer on the basis of a Data Sheet of Technical Information Sheet supplied to the customer, which describes the properties of the material.

As it is unlikely that the Toll Manufacturer will generate a Data Sheet for a Toll Manufactured product and as there is a need for more detailed formal agreement with the customer another approach must be adopted.

This agreement should take place at the earliest opportunity, and should include both product and process specifications. Not only does this prevent any disputes arising at a later date, but simplifies the process of contract review which I'll mention later.

Part of that formal agreement should include exact details of any inspection, test and analytical methods used either in-process or for final product verification.

Solution

My experience is that the best way to formalise the product and process specifications is to compile all the necessary documentation e.g.

Batch Sheets, including formulation and manufacturing procedure.
Process control sheets, including details of in-process testing required.
Final product specifications including analytical methods
Etc.

and ask the customer to sign and date each document.

Again, my experience is that the customer will appreciate the amount of professionalism being taken to meet his exact requirements.

The stage at which the formal agreement takes place will depend on a number of factors, for example the amount of R & D work required, the progression from laboratory through pilot plant onto main plant etc.

It may well be that the agreement is 'provisional' until either a pilot plant or main plant batch is produced - nevertheless there should be a formal agreement.

Just to give you an idea of the kind of detail required in the documentation I'd like to give you an example from my own experience.

One of the areas where Baxenden seem to be using a large number of different test methods is for the determination of TOTAL SOLIDS CONTENT on solution polymers. Depending on the end use of the product the test method can vary considerably - at one time we were using 9 different solids methods for different customers.

So what was the problem? Well, Baxenden had taken on a Toll Manufacturing job for a polymer in solution, gone through the development stages into the pilot plant and sent a sample of pilot plant production for customer approval.

The material was tested by the customer who came back to us saying it was 2% low in solids.

We had received the analytical and test methods from the customer and as far as we could tell were using the correct procedure - temperature, time, sample weight and achieving a result in specification.

After discussions with the customer we eventually found out that the disposable aluminium dishes we were using for our solids determinations were approximately half the diameter of those used by our customer.

Tests quickly confirmed that the problem was solvent retention in the smaller dishes.

Perhaps that gives an idea of the kind of detail required. We should have asked the right question at the time - we certainly do now! The same comment applies to any other test method, of course.

It is probably worth mentioning here that there are essentially two different types of Toll Manufacturing to consider:-

(i) Where the customer supplies a full formulation, manufacturing method, product specification etc. - everything you need, only minimal R & D input may be required.

and

(ii) Where the customer is seeking either a product or material without supplying any information other than a specification (perhaps a tentative one) or the customer is seeking a 'performance' or 'effect' material.

Clearly in the second case the Toll Manufacturer has to do a significant amount of R & D work to achieve the desired product or material.

This is particularly true in the case of 'performance' materials such as polymers which is the area I'm particularly familiar with. In that case it is quite likely that it will be the Toll Manufacturer that proposes a formulation and specification to the customer rather than the reverse being the case.

However, the same procedure for formally agreeing specifications should still be followed.

Problem 4. Can you fulfil any special customer requirements?

Like the last point concerning formal agreement of details with the customer I consider this also to be a very important point.

Many customers will have special requirements of Toll Manufacturers.

They may require that their own labels are used for the finished product, special containers or container markings may be specified, or that their own batch numbers be used on the finished product.

There may be a requirement to supply SPC information, or the process may fall into the 'Special Process' category i.e. one where the characteristics of the product can only be fully evaluated in the customers end-product or process.

The customer may therefore require a batch sample along with all in-process and final product analytical results before acceptance of the product.

All these requests must be catered for while maintaining traceability within the quality system and meeting the requirements of contract review.

Solution

The system must be capable of ensuring that the information necessary to meet the customers requirements, which could be either part of the agreed specification package (e.g. use customers labels) or be on an order-to-order basis (e.g. customer batch numbers) goes to the correct location to enable the necessary action to be taken.

In these days of computerised everything this is not too difficult to achieve but needs careful thought.

In common with other companies Baxenden uses a computerised system for the generation of batch and process control sheets, test and analytical information etc. as well as for Sales Orders.

My preference for ensuring the appropriate requirements for the customer are met is to use a 'two tier' system in the documentation.

The first 'tier' is for 'standing instructions' and can form either part of the batch sheet documentation of the Sales Order - these standing instructions will cater for requirements such as container type, customers own labels etc.

This information is normally not changed and will form part of the original documentation formally agreed with the customer.

The second 'tier' is for variable instructions which form part of the Sales Order documentation - these instructions will cater for requirements such as customers own batch bumbers, container markings etc.

This information is entered on an order-to-order basis as required by the customers order.

Provided the documents are then passed to the appropriate person, the necessary actions can then be taken.

Problem 5.   Do you have facilities available for the storage, verification and maintenance of purchaser supplied product?

For Toll Manufacturing, many customers prefer to supply raw materials Free of Charge.

Facilities must be available for the storage (segregated if necessary), and testing of such supplies.

It is the manufacturers responsibility to have the systems to track the material through the manufacturing process.

The manufacturer is also responsible for recording deviation in quality and yield from those contracted - as well as any losses that may occur due to spillage etc. of the purchaser supplied material. He must account fully for use of the material.

It should be noted that, just because the material is supplied by the customer, it does not absolve the manufacturer from the responsibility of ensuring that the material is fit to use.

Solution

If necessary, separate or segregated storage facilities will be required for purchaser supplied product. The required procedures for enabling the material to be inspected/tested will also need to be installed, although it is quite likely that the existing quality system will cope with this.

Problem 6. Do you have facilities available for storage
of finished product?

It may be that the required storage conditions for
the Toll Manufactured product are substantially different
from those the supplier normally uses e.g. refrigerated
storage may be required.

Solution

Finished product storage conditions should form part
of the specification 'document' package originally agreed
with the customer.

Problem 7. What about changes to processes or raw material
sources?

For 'own-products' an in-house R & D facility will be
able to assess the effect that changes to manufacturing
processes or different sources of raw materials will have
on a finished product.

That is not necessarily the case in a Toll Manufacturing job as it is not uncommon for the Toll Manufacturer
to be unaware of the end use of a product or be unfamiliar
with a particular product area.

The product could be an intermediate which will go
on to have other processes or reactions carried out on it.
Hence the Toll Manufacturer may not be in a position to
determine the effect of changes to processes or raw materials.

Solution

Customer approval must always be sought for any
changes relating to the product no matter how minor they
appear to the Toll Manufacturer.

Having said that, it may well be the case that for
performance or effect materials, where the Toll Manufacturer
has been involved with a substantial amount of R &D work
to arrive at the end product that he may be in a better
position to advise on any effects due to changes in processes or raw materials.

However customer approval must still be sought before
any changes are made.

Problem 8. What about Contract Review?

Contract review is particularly important for Toll Manufacturing operations.   Specifically:-

(a) Can the customer's order for Toll Manufactured
product be cross referenced to the formally agreed specification?

It is not uncommon for customers to order under a product code/description that is not necessarily the same as that of the formally agreed specification, manufacturers internal codes could have been used - the Contract Review process must cope with such eventualities and provide objective evidence linking any such differences.

(b)   The ability to meet other customer requirements e.g. customers own batch nos., labels, container markings, certificates etc. must fall within the scope of the Contract Review Process.

Solution

I've already mentioned, when I was talking about 'Special Customer Requirements', the procedure I favour to achieve a satisfactory Contract Review System.

Problem 9.   Are you prepared for customer audits?

Most manufacturers registered to ISO 9002 will be familiar with customer audits.   The occasional customer for 'own products' does ask if he can come and audit the suppliers quality system, not very frequently in my experience, although I must admit it's happening more than it used to.

In the case of Toll Manufacturing however, it is my experience that the majority of customers perform not only detailed quality audits of their suppliers, but safety and environmental audits as well.

It's also likely that the customer will want to send a representative to 'Oversee' the first batch being manufactured.   This must be achieved with regard to the commercial secrecy of other processes that may be ongoing at the same time.

Solution

Be prepared to have your system well and truly vetted!

General

As a last 'general' comment, it would seem wise for the Technical Sales or Commercial Manager responsible for gaining or controlling Toll Manufacturing business and who is the main contact with the customer to have a thorough understanding of the quality system - he will then be able to see potential problems and resolve them before they arise.

You've probably noticed that there are a number of areas normally within the scope of ISO 9002 that I have not mentioned.

e.g. calibration of measuring and test equipment, purchasing etc.

The simple reason is that those areas should present few, if any problems. The normal quality system applies.

In conclusion

So, are the points I've made and the problems I've mentioned obvious?

Well, yes they probably are - once you've spotted them.

But spotting them - preferably before they lead to difficulties is the challenging bit!

As you will probably gather, there are a number of hurdles to be jumped on a Toll Manufacturing job. For 'own products', some of the hurdles are missing and others are familiar - the 'normal' quality system will cope with them.

All of the points should be borne in mind from the very start when considering a new Toll Manufacturing job.

Whilst the Toll Manufacturer may be fully prepared to spend some cash in, say, buying an additional piece of measuring or test equipment, he may not be so keen to invest a large sum of money in a refrigerated warehouse - so if you're likely to need one it would be useful to find out at the outset, not after a lot of effort has been expended and the MD says you can't have one - it's best to look far ahead and get all the facts at the earliest opportunity.

Well, as I said at the start it's a question of attention to detail.

That's true of ISO 9002 in general but even greater attention to detail is, in my opinion, required for a system coping with Toll Manufacturing.

Total Quality—Total Partnership

W. A. Christmas and J. M. Rugg

ICI CHEMICALS & POLYMERS LTD., RUNCORN, CHESHIRE WA7 4QG, UK

1   SUMMARY

This paper outlines some of the quality management issues which ICI Chemicals and Polymers Ltd have addressed to ensure the agreed requirements of its customers are achieved at all times. It also examines the close link between this objective and the requirement to provide society with sufficient evidence of ICI's ability to operate safe logistics services with "responsible care" having due regard to the environment in which it operates.

2   INTRODUCTION

ICI Chemicals and Polymers Limited is one of the main Business Groups of Imperial Chemical Industries PLC. ICI C&P comprises several businesses representing the Petrochemicals, Plastics, Chemical Products, Chlor Chemicals and Performance Chemicals interests of ICI PLC. The Distribution Services Group of ICI C&P provides and procures a full range of services for the above Businesses and offers functional support to other parts of ICI Businesses located in UK and Europe, namely ICI Materials, ICI Specialties and European Vinyls Corporation.

The UK and Europe represent approx 49% of the ICI PLC Group Sales whilst for C&P the same market accounts for 85% of sales. In distribution terms this translates into over 600,000 consignments per annum; the majority of which are despatched from the two main production centres of Teesside and Merseyside.

3   CUSTOMER FOCUS

ICI C&P has fostered Quality Partnerships with key distribution suppliers to improve the capability of distribution systems.

Key Indicators are used to monitor performance and

promote continuous improvement.

The focus on external customers by the internal customer supplier chain is being extended to 'Partners'. Joint Missions and factors critical for success, recognise that the future of such partnerships depends upon the prosperity and success of its customers.

4   FOCUS ON CUSTOMER SERVICE REQUIREMENTS

Within ICI C&P, Quality management initiatives have been introduced not only to ensure survival and growth but to drive towards the goal of delivering and continuously improving the provision of the safest and the best possible service to customers.

During the late 1970's and early 1980's, 90% of ICI C&P's business for packaged chemicals consisted of full loads, with small lots mainly available via independent stockists or distributors. Changes in customers' purchasing strategies, often reducing the number of suppliers, required ICI C&P to change its policies. Small loads now account for approximately 35% of movements, increasing to 80% in sóme particular product/market sectors. In the case of bulk liquids the effect is not so dramatic but there is an increasing demand for "mini" bulk deliveries of specialty chemicals in loads as small as 5 tonnes. The increasing number of cutomers in Continental Europe and growth in requirement for "just in time deliveries" pose a particular challenge.

This requires a keen and sharp focus on the service agreements ICI C&P negotiates with its transport and associated distribution suppliers. Progress towards achieving the best possible service is vital for us, and a pre-requisite to gaining new business on the European mainland as well as in the UK. Customers no longer accept distance as a reason for failing to meet delivery requirements. Moves towards "Quality Partnerships" are necessary if we are to provide customer satisfaction and achieve prosperity for all parties involved. Recognition of the importance of a reliable distribution service link is key to the survival and growth of all in the supplier -customer chain.

5   FOCUS ON SAFETY AND ENVIRONMENT

The Chemical Industry is bound by a "Licence to Operate" within the community. This encompasses not only the locations where chemicals are produced or consumed, but also transit between them. The public in general, and certain sectors in particular, are increasingly critical of the chemical industry and its operations.

The public image of the chemical industry is often

unsatisfactory and the power to effect change rests with us. The public increasingly expects our industry, its suppliers and many of its customers to reduce and eventually cease any pollution of the environment. The transport industry is closely involved with the safe handling and disposal of residues and washings from road tanks and tank containers. This is one of many areas where increasing attention and investment will have to be given to satisfy the requirements of society.

We must strive to achieve and be recognised as providers of a safe distribution and storage service. Equally we must reassure the public that there is a totally satisfactory system of quality management controls which minimise the threat of chemical hazards during the transportation of our products.

6   COSTS AND EFFICIENCY

Many of the businesses within ICI Chemical & Polymers require customer requirements to be met at the lowest cost-effective distribution charge without minimising safety or service. This demands very competitive prices per unit load, coupled with the highest possible payload and the efficient scheduling and utilisation of equipment. The balance between higher investment and lower rates can present major difficulties but provides an excellent incentive for considering the formation of Quality Partnerships between the chemical, haulage and associated logistics industries.

7   LEGISLATIVE

The UK Government's apparent refusal to move from 38 tonne to 40 tonne GVW puts UK based Businesses at a dis-advantage. If not addressed, the higher freight costs per tonne, will disadvantage us compared to our Continental competitors. This weight penalty effectively reduces the UK payload potential by approx 10% and reinforces the earlier argument about ensuring investment in the best possible equipment to ensure maximum payloads. ICI C&P has to provide a better than first class customer service in order to retain and grow its business in Continental Europe. The regular monitoring of service levels using quality measurement, is one of the essential steps ICI C&P has taken jointly with distribution suppliers to focus upon customer needs and monitor its performance in all markets.

8   QUALITY FOR THE 1990'S

Since the creation of ICI C&P in 1987 a quality improvement process has been pursued, focusing upon customers and seeking continuous improvement in everything the company produces or performs. A lot has been learnt about total quality, how it can be best applied, what improvements can be made and how these can be implemented to take us towards a standard of providing the best imaginable products and services.

The ICI C&P Quality Improvement Process recognises the future success and prosperity of any business relationship is dependent upon the prosperity and success of its customers. A Quality vision promoting the existence of an interdependent relationship, extending along a customer chain from raw materials suppliers through manufacturing and business support processes, including distribution activities, was produced to focus upon both the internal and external perspective.

This vision for the future is based upon four basic principles.

1   Continuous Improvement is natural.
2   We have systems to assure Quality.
3   Measurement is used automatically to test
     performance and progress.
4   The ultimate aim is to <u>delight</u> customers not just
     satisfy basic needs.

Communication of the quality vision within C&P, required every member of staff to effect a change in their behaviour and adopt the above principles which require everyone to operate differently.

Education programmes for all staff needed to be more than just statements of principle. In-house training focused on Quality Processes and the need for continuing action at all levels using an agreed framework to effect change with leadership from the top of the organisation.

Leadership of the quality process within ICI C&P is provided by the Chief Executive as chairman of the Quality Strategy Management Group, constituted from General Managers of individual business groups and support functions. General Managers chair local steering committees which are responsible for the implementation of the C&P eight step quality improvement process. They each determine local strategy, monitor progress and report back to the strategy management group using a series of defined measurement criteria. The tactical arms of the steering committees are typically five to eight quality improvement teams operating within each business or function. Cascading from the improvement teams are corrective action teams, work groups, peer groups, common interest groups etc all dealing with continuous improvement at local and cross-functional levels. Management Teams are supported by Quality Managers, Co-ordinators and QA Managers who assist Line Managers with implementation of the improvement process and Quality Training.

9   THE EIGHT STEP PROCESS

There are eight things C&P feel it needs to have in place
in order to provide a robust Quality Improvement process,
these are:-

-    Commitment at senior level and all levels with regular
     visible reinforcement.
-    A Quality Organisation to make quality improvement happ
     that ultimately becomes the line management itself.
-    Awareness and Education programmes to produce speedy
     implementation.
-    Measurement to be displayed that facilitates meaningful
     improvement.
-    A structure for each business/support function/operatin
     unit to aid and promote improvement efforts.
-    Management of key processes and systems using QA as a
     start towards a future of viable systems management.
-    Use of the ideas generated and recognition of people's
     contributions.
-    Confidence of our progress in quality improvement by
     implementing effective monitoring and auditing
     mechanisms.

     This is 'Defined in more detail in Appendix 2.'

10   SERVICE LEVELS

Each department or operating unit is required to define its
process and Quality management system, obtain QA
Registration to ISO 9000 (145 todate). Agreements are made
with external and internal suppliers and customers on the
type and level of service required to support the needs of
external customers. Service standards have been defined
and typically for a sales and distribution area these could
be:-

Quality of Delivery

     Every customer will receive the required product in
the correct place at the agreed time and all staff involved
in the physical movement (ICI and external contractors)
will be polite, helpful and efficient.
     Non-Conformances in Customer Service. All departments
will have an agreed procedure for dealing with customer
complaints and non-conformances of ICI's service to its
customers. The customer will be told of the proposed
course of action for correction and improvement, its
timescale and informed promptly of any deviation from
this course.

11   DISTRIBUTION SERVICES CASE HISTORY
     (Use of Quality Service Indicators)

Distribution Services, as an internal supplier to the
Product Business Group within the customer chain, worked

with the Sales Departments, analysed customer complaints as required under registered quality assured systems, categorised these into various types and noted that 60% were distribution related.

The majority of the 'distribution' category were connected with late or early delivery problems. These were analysed down to the individual suppliers of distribution services, which started the process of moving towards more clearly defined service level agreements with external suppliers to reflect the agreements ICI C&P had made with its external customers.

Quality assurance having been obtained was not taken as an excuse to relax by managers of the distribution areas but was, and still is, actively used as a catalyst to encourage continuous motivation of management and staff to improve the systems and processes they operate and control. External suppliers were encouraged to examine their own quality management processes and seek QA accreditation in their own right to promote a greater understanding for the need to focus upon customer requirements and reach agreements to sustain service levels.

The monitoring of service levels used 2 key indicators; customer complaints and/or non-conformances deviating from the agreed standards with suppliers. In time, techniques became more sophisticated but results continued to be reported and displayed as simple histograms and bar charts to the haulier etc providing the service, followed by meetings to discuss joint action for improvements.

With transport companies beginning to analyse their own performance under QA and TQM policies, more regular meetings were held tackling not only problems identified by the ICI C&P measurement process but those faced by the hauliers in loading and delivering the product. This produced a two-way process, often self-generating and moving towards a total quality culture. This culture encouraged ICI to seek criticism and comments on its own attitudes and activities, further promoting the processes of measurement and continuous improvement at all levels within both sets of organisations.

Closer relationships have developed with hauliers leading towards the first class service defined and sought. Quality partnerships began to evolve and the process with some groups of suppliers has now reached the stage of joint ICI C&P/supplier quality training activities. A "meeting of minds" on success factors critical for the business is leading towards "Joint Missions" and an acceptance of the need for a customer focused culture recognising the importance of customer prosperity.

This work is being been extended into promoting closer relationships with shipping lines, warehousing companies and package manufacturers. It forms the framework within which all businesses in ICI C&P are developing their approach to future business with the customer base.

12   THE FUTURE

ICI C&P Distribution Services will require:-

All suppliers to be accredited to ISO 9000 or equivalent. A reduction in our supplier base and the formation of quality partnerships with key suppliers.

The use of Quality management processes and systems to ensure supplier/customer requirements are fully agreed and understood by all parts of the customer chain and at every level of employee within participating organisations. Continuous monitoring of performance and analysis of the resulting data is used to seek and implement continuous improvement.

Together, these form the basis of an action plan for a joint commitment to focusing on the requirements and continuous prosperity of the customer, the suppliers and the communities within which they operate.

Success will only be achieved through the participation of us all in Total Quality Management.

APPENDIX 1   - The Quality Vision of ICI Chemicals
               and Polymers Ltd
APPENDIX 2   - The Eight Things to do

APPENDIX 1

THE QUALITY VISION OF ICI CHEMICALS AND POLYMERS LTD

We delight customers by anticipating needs and exceeding expectations.

Continuous systematic improvement is our way of life.

The world sees us as a strong, successful company, the industry leaders.

We judge ourselves against the highest of standards.

"Partnership" is our way of doing business, and everyone benefits.

Teamwork and trust are the hallmarks of our organisation.

Our company is renowned for its capable and caring people.

We have pride in our jobs and know we are valued. Personal growth is actively encouraged.

The community takes pride in our presence. Society values our contribution.

Measurement is widely used and always valued.

APPENDIX 2

THE EIGHT THINGS TO DO

1   Sustain Commitment

Sustaining commitment is vital to the success of the Quality Improvement Process and requires a sincere, single-minded and enthusiastic approach. Unless everyone believes wholeheartedly in the process that leads to total quality and in the values embodied in the vision of the future for ICI Chemicals & Polymers, then the benefits will not follow. The key is being able to sustain commitment throughout the team — but to do that successfully requires a thorough understanding of quality improvement.

2   Organise for Quality

Without the right organisation, the standard of quality and service which ICI C&P seeks to achieve for its customers will never be attained. Quality needs to be managed: to commit resources, to focus our energy and to encourage everyone to take part. Quality improvement is a long-haul process and requires time and effort. Visible, active organisation is essential and is provided throughout C&P by Quality Steering Groups, Quality Improvement Teams, Quality Managers, Corrective Actions Teams and local work groups — in short, every single one of us.

3   Create Awareness and Education Programmes

Education and awareness programmes are the bedrock of the Quality Improvement Process. They establish the right environment for sustained quality improvement by creating common understanding and belief, and a common language. Simple tools and techniques help us do our jobs more effectively and enable us to solve the problems that we can do something about ourselves. That gives us courage and confidence and puts the vision of quality into a practical context.

4   Develop the Measurement Habit

Measurement provides the only certain, objective test of whether quality is improving since it provides comparisons with past performance and can be contrasted with best practice. Measurement helps in assigning priorities and, by revealing the true capability of our systems, it reveals the progress we are making. Managers must lead by example and everyone must be trained in measurement techniques to derive continual improvement throughout the organisation. As well as looking inwards, we should encourage external measurement against the features of the very best organisations, in any business sphere.

5   Structure Improvement Opportunities

Without a clearly understood process, quality improvement will be, at best, piecemeal. Formalising the process and communicating it throughout the workplace helps to focus more effectively the efforts being made to move towards best imaginable practices. This structured approach enables complaints to be handled properly, suggestions to be acted upon and problems to be solved. A robust feedback mechanism ensures that these lessons, once learnt, can be shared and time and resources allocated to make certain that improvement becomes part of everyone's job.

6   Manage Systems

The Quality Improvement Process needs to be under-pinned by the systems of the organisation in order to delight our customers with the services we provide. ISO 9000 is a crucial element of our quality process and ICI Chemicals & Polymers was the first company in the world to achieve 100 ISO 9000 registrations. But our systems need to be continuously improved and simplified to sustain our vital competitive edge.

7   Involve and Recognise

Everyone needs to be involved in improvement and should be actively encouraged and supported in this. Our organisation has a wealth and talent which we should use to find better ways of doing things. Involvement and recognition are about realising and valuing the potential of everyone within the organisation. Openly respecting the contribution of everyone has direct impact on how we deal with our customers.

8   Audit and Review Progress

Systematic operations are needed to review the Quality Improvement Process at all levels. They reveal how the quality process is progressing and help keep improvement on course. The existence of audit and review procedures shows that an organisation is serious about its vision to achieve Total Quality. Audits enable us to hold the gains and reviews help us to set new goals. Audit and review procedures allow an organisation to improve continuously its approach to quality improvement – an approach that should never stand still.

Haulage: The Transport Company Perspective

R. A. Kirby

LINKMAN TANKERS LTD., NAB LANE, BIRSTALL, BATLEY, WEST YORKSHIRE WF17 9NH, UK

Linkman is a £35m a year turnover subsidiary of the
Transport Division of the Transport Development Group
Plc, a major European distribution and logistics
Company. It operates as an autonomous unit with full
profit responsibility. The management team is charged
with ensuring compliance with all legislative, environmental and other requirements serving its customer base
through 700 staff using 450 vehicles, operating from
five major depots mainly for the oil and chemical
industries.

Until June 1990 three separate and very different
organisations operated the businesses that are now
Linkman. During the ensuing period we have had to pull
together all the disparate parts and cultures to create
a new persona. This has included rationalisation and
consequent redundancies. We have had to create a
single BS5750 quality system where previously three
existed. This in itself was a major task although
well worthwhile as it tested the management review
procedures to the limit.

Early in 1991 Transport Development Group itself went
through a major re-organisation following a complete
strategic review. One of the most vital issues to come
from this was the adoption of a statement of intent.
This was that TDG should become:-

     The best logistics company in Europe:

          best for its   customers

          best for its   shareholders

     and best for its   people.

This is in turn reflected in Linkman's own main objective of being the preferred supplier of bulk fluid distribution services in the UK - the natural choice for all our existing and future customers.

The Linkman Quality Policy Statement expands on this philosophy:

> We will be seen by our customers to offer a service which shows us to be the quality leader among the companies with whom we compete.
>
> We will put quality and safety first in everything we do.
>
> We will be the most cost effective supplier of services among the companies with whom we compete.
>
> We will constantly improve our services by setting ourselves annual targets of improvement in the quality of everything we do.
>
> We will involve all our people, developing their skills and abilities, and using those skills and abilities in support of our Quality Policy.

The pursuit of these ideals is the minimum qualification necessary for us to contemplate partnerships with our customers.

When the idea was first mooted of applying BS5750 to a haulage company, people had difficulty in conceiving of the relevance of the standard to the form of operations that we had. This was perhaps as much a factor of the jargon used in the actual BS5750 Part II document as anything else.

Once the light started to dawn reactions varied from cynicism, a feeling that "we were already quality" to a belief that our customers had come up with yet another device to nail us to the floor, especially on haulage rates!

Very few understood at that stage the long term implications of the initiative or the benefits that could potentially be derived from it once it had been fully embraced and become engrained in our businesses.

In reality very few have yet made significant progress in fully developing TQM in their companies and some still take a jaundiced view of the whole process. They do so at their peril.

We all operate in an increasingly competitive and more and more international market. If we are to prosper in our chosen areas of activity we must all be more professional and better at what we do.

To achieve this we must be clearly focused on the issues which will enable us not only to survive, but to thrive in what is and doubtless will remain, a bracing economic environment.

The prime objective obviously has to be to satisfy or, better still, to delight our customers. It has already been illustrated that this key issue is well in focus at Linkman, although the developing and printing of the picture is far from complete and much more difficult.

Listening to and understanding exactly what it is that customers really want is not easy, but the only chance we have of satisfying the requirement is if we have that complete understanding of all the facts and needs.

Having agreed the requirement we then have to develop solutions that are safe, practical, cost effective and also, possibly, innovative.

In our industry safety has always been high on the agenda, it can be no other way, but there is always room for improvement. If in the 25m miles the Linkman fleet travels each year we have one accident or incident, however minor, it is one too many. The measurement and display tools that are integral in total quality solutions have an invaluable role to play here. Incidentially, it is still the case that there has only been one fatality on the roads of the UK in the last 24 years as a direct consequence of the carriage of hazardous chemicals in bulk, a record which we must do all we can to protect.

The environmental agenda is having an ever increasing influence on our activities and whilst we may see it as a nuisance in some of its manifestations, we have to address all of the issues that are raised. The topics such as tank cleaning and the safe disposal of toxic wastes therefrom cannot be ignored and very substantial investment will be needed to overcome the problems. It may be that for certain products we have to accept dedication of tanks for their movement and the consequent increase in costs.

Of course, cost is obviously another major factor. We do appreciate that to remain competitive in world markets our customers must have the lowest cost base possible and we, as an industry, have a very important role to play in this area. We are convinced that the application of the principles of total quality will ultimately yield substantial cost benefits in which we can all share, but it will take time, a scarce commodity in the market. There appears to be plenty of scope for the use of TQM techniques in this area!

Innovation is the most exciting issue and potentially
the area that can give us all the greatest yield in
the long term.

New thinking can be applied to virtually everything
that we do and it is worth mentioning just a few of the
potential areas for innovation in the transport and
distribution industry.

> Training, motivation and, if you will forgive
> the Americanism, compensation packages.

> Multi-skilled operatives; drivers that can also
> service their vehicles, complete with the aid of
> technology their administration and, most
> importantly, look after customers.

> New operational parameters to maximise utilisation
> of expensive resources.

> Technology for load traceability to provide both
> environmental and customer service benefits.

> Use of advanced material in vehicle design to
> help maximise payload. The average 38 tonne
> vehicle still weighs 14 tonnes without a load.

> Increased use of multi-modal opportunities
> utilising rail or even canals to minimise
> environmental impact and, hopefully, save costs.

The list is virtually endless and in terms of implementation we have hardly begun.

Probably the single most important factor in the
success or otherwise of any enterprise is the human
resource - the people.

When Linkman was launched in July 1990 we brought as
many of our employees together in one place as was
possible and involved them in a presentation of the
new company entitled "People Are Our Future".

This belief is fundamental and it applies not only to
management, but to all employees whatever their role
in the organisation. It is only through people that
we can achieve our objectives; by selecting the right
people in the first instance and then training them,
motivating them and adequately rewarding them for what
they do in the enterprise. Above all, we must respect
them and involve them in all of the processes relating
to the development of the company.

It is for this reason that the term "Total Quality
Management" is a bit of a misnomer because whilst the
management is a vital part of the whole, it is only a
part, perhaps this is why different labels have been

given to quality initiatives in various organisations;
"continuous improvement programmes" or "customer
satisfaction initiatives". Similar names will actually
broaden the focus of the quality drive by clearly
implying that it is not just a management initiative,
but a cultural change to involve every employee and to
widen the responsibility for success to all of those
who can in reality have a degree of influence.

The problems of introducing total quality in transport
are different from those in many other businesses. In
the main we have a nomadic workforce, it is not easy
to get groups of drivers together to talk about any
issue, let alone quality. One response when we do
discuss the matter with drivers is "what about the
plant operators that are more concerned about their tea
break or the end of their shift. They are not concerned
about the driver". Nor are they bothered about the
costs of standing an £80,000 vehicle for two hours.
This type of attitude conveys totally wrong messages
to drivers and is an area that we, as hauliers, can
see a need for enormous improvement both at production
sites and at storage terminals.

When you think about what your haulier provides for you
perhaps issues such as this become more relevant. The
vehicle is the packaging for your product, the driver
is your representative every time he pulls onto your
customer's premises. He probably sees your customer
far more regularly than your sales force. He and his
vehicle can possibly affect your success or otherwise
with a customer at least as much as your commercial
decisions, your salesman or even, in some instances,
product quality. So he is an important guy who we
should all perhaps look at with a fresh pair of eyes.

By and large, tanker drivers are a very competent and
committed bunch of people. In Linkman we view them as
potentially our greatest asset, along with our
traffic, administration and workshop staff. We do
really believe that people are our future, and yours
too!

How do we tackle quality and other issues springing
from it? As stated earlier that it is not just a
management issue, it has to start from the management.
What we do and say is absolutely vital because as
commented when illustrating attitudes to drivers on
plants, it is all too easy to convey wrong messages to
people.

If the Managing director turns up for work in a filthy
car, an old, stained suit and scruffy shoes he can
hardly chastise a driver for his or his vehicle's
unsightly appearance. He has already decided what sort
of outfit he works for.

The important issue for managers is to recognise that
before trying to introduce total quality into an
organisation they have to alter some of their behaviour
patterns. They should not underestimate the amount of
sheer hard work that will be necessary to actually
change both the way they themselves think and act and
also those that work for or with them.

Within our company we are just embarking on a programme
of management development to train all of our managers
down to supervisor level in how to handle the
processes of a total quality initiative. This activity
has started with the help of external consultants who
have undertaken a survey of employee attitudes and
assisted us to understand some of the issues in the
business that we need to address. In other words, a
"swat" analysis.

From this base we are running a series of workshops
to evaluate the requirements for change in attitudes,
communications, motivation, etc., and also to improve
the team working skills of the management.

Once we have been through this period of training we
should have achieved three things.

   1. All of our management team will better
       understand what we want the company to be and
       to do. They will also be committed to
       achieving these objectives.

   2. We will also understand what we as individuals
      need to do to guarantee the attainment of our
      ultimate goals.

   3. We will understand how we can enable all of
      our employees to appreciate and be involved
      in the change process needed to effectively
      instil total quality into every aspect of the
      business.

It must be the case that a non-confrontational approach
to business where all parties specify their needs and
where people work together to meet those aspirations
is a better one than where ethics and honesty are
ignored and the "dog eat dog" philosophy thrives.
We sincerely hope this is the case.

Many years ago a school had both a house motto and
school motto.

   The first was:

   "United we stand, divided we fall"

   and the second:

"Aut vincere, aut mori", Either to conquer or die.

Both are very apt in the present context!

Quality System Certification for Chemical Industry on a World Wide Basis

N. A. Chichger

BRITISH STANDARDS INSTITUTION, P.O. BOX 375, MILTON KEYNES MK14 6LL, UK

The Need for Quality and Adoption of QA by the UK Chemical Industry

The recession in the early 1980's drove home several important lessons to Chemical companies. The need for internal efficiency in all aspects of the company's operations was one. Another important lesson, was the paramount need to satisfy the customer in quality, reliability and delivery. In fact, in total service.

In doing business around the world, particularly in the US and Japan, Chemical companies found that customers were increasingly asking for assurance from their suppliers about quality management, as part of their own programmes to improve quality. The first to get these messages were Chemical companies supplying into the electronics, motor vehicle and off shore oil industries together with those concerned with medicines or defence contracts. Slowly but surely "quality" became a much wider and more positive concept than just having a Quality Control Laboratory. It embraced all activities of the business, working together to assure that the quality of product or service would satisfy all of the customer's requirements.

The need for this approach in Industry was recognised in the UK by the Government and promoted in its White Paper.

"Standards, Quality and International Competitiveness"

The UK Chemical Industry took very little notice of BS5750 when it was first published. The Standard appeared to be written for the Engineering Industry, there were fears of bureaucratic procedures, and most people felt that Quality may simply be the "flavour of the month".

Up until early 1987 there were effectively no UK Chemical Companies registered to ISO9000. Presently there are over 600 companies registered. What has brought about this rapid embrace of the standard by the Industry?

4 major factors have contributed to this

: Demand by customers, led by the Car Industry, for their suppliers to become Quality Assured.

: Acceptance by the Chemical Industries Association that there was a need to become pro-active in promoting and "interpreting the Standard in the form of published Guidelines.

: General realisation by the Industry that the benefits of Quality Assurance are real and positive (and is not just because "If that is what the customer wants then we had better do it").

: Self propagating style of the Standard which demands from your supplier that same standard to which you operate. Your suppliers are usually other Chemical companies.

On the last point some of you no doubt have been receiving demands by your customers that you meet these certain standards.

The rapid acceptance of Quality Assurance by the UK Industry has been achieved by two routes:

: Those companies, notably the larger ones, who have adopted Total Quality Management as a company philosophy, have sold it as a company project to each and every part of the company structure, starting at the top, and have certification to ISO9000 as a step (albeit an important one) on the long road to Total Quality Management.

: Others, notably the smaller to medium sized Companies, have set out deliberately to seek only ISO9000 registration and when they have achieved this have said, "Let's target for Total Quality Management".

Either route is valid for they have the same end. Both however demand two things:

: There is full and meaningful commitment by the Chief Executive.

: ISO9000 is seen as a part of the whole overall philosophy and not an end in its own right.

Some of the benefits from a commitment to Total Quality
Management, as reported by BSI QA registered companies include:

:   Failure rates - down significantly (consequent savings in
    plant time and management time).

:   Shop Floor awareness of and interest in business performance.

:   Supplier performance improvement.

:   Customer service improvement in product consistency and
    delivery.

:   Competitive edge over non-certificated users.

As companies progress down the road to Total Quality Management,
it ultimately embraces all departments:

:   Finance

:   Personnel

:   Research and Development

:   Engineering workshops, etc

as well as the production and selling functions.

How does the Mechanism of Certification Operate in the UK

There are 14 Accredited Certification Bodies in the UK prepared
to examine a Company to ISO9000 Standard and grants its
registration. 4 bodies active in Chemical Industry BSI, LEQA,
YQAF and Bureau Veritas.

These Certification Bodies are accredited by a Government
controlled body called the NACCB (National Accreditation Council
for Certification Bodies) to ensure that consistency of
interpretation of the standard and working practices of
certification Bodies; BSI QA (not to be confused with BSI, which
is the UK National Standard setting Authority) is one of the
accredited Certification Bodies in UK.

To summarise, the mechanics of the certification process and how
it is operated by BSI QA refer to Appendix 1 (Route to
registration). On successful completion of assessment, the
applicant company will thereafter be visited at random intervals
without warning to enable recheck of the company's procedures
with particular emphasis on weaker areas. The certification Body
can remove a Company's registration although time is usually
given to correct areas of major non-conformance. Certification
allows you to publicly promote that you are an ISO9000 Registered
Firm using a registered logo.

BSI QA for historical reasons in the area of Chemical Industry Certification.

Since the original standard was written for the Engineering Industry, this has had to be "interpreted" by the issue of a document called "The CIA/BSI ISO9000 - 1987 Guidelines" which effectively translates the Standard where necessary into more readily understandable phrases pertinent to the Chemical Industry's technology and language. These Guidelines are in many ways the definitive interpreted Standard for the Industry.

These Guidelines have now been accepted, with some amendments, by CEFIC (Conseil European Des Federations de L'Industrie Chimique) and are entitled "CEFIC Guidelines to EN29001.

In order that there shall be ongoing overseeing of the Standard and an ability to answer questions of clarification and understanding, there exists a BSI QA Certification Authority charged with this guardianship role for the Chemical and Allied Industries. This committee consists of representatives from Industry customers or their Trade Associations, the CIA and from BSI QA. This committee meets regularly, debates interpretation, gives clarification and gives direction so that the standard is kept live to the changing needs and ways in which the Chemical Industry operates.

THE EUROPEAN SCENE

Within the UK Chemical Industry, more and more its customers are outside the UK, its suppliers and often its major suppliers are outside the UK and that it is truly an International Industry. To look on any Quality Assurance impacts in an insular way is very short sighted - it is the international impact that must dominate. Quality Assurance is here to stay, the benefits are real, particularly on an International Scale. Quality Assurance will evolve to include topics like product liability and insurance and responsible environmental care.

The UK industry thus seeks with its European partners, actively to find a common quality mechanism under which we can all operate, and not just a standard that we have in ISO9000. What we seek is a way in which to develop a real and meaningful confidence in each others certification mechanisms. This is being done through an organisation called EQNET (European Quality system Certification Network). BSI QA is a member of this network. All signatories are committed to developing bilateral agreements with other signatories. The principle is one of strong cooperation as the basis of providing a pan-European certification service. Members of EQNET are, therefore, not competing for business in each others country but will carry out assessment and/or certification in another country if specifically requested by the applicant. Prior to entering into these agreements with other EQNET signatories an evaluation of the other signatory's system has been conducted to ensure that it operates in accordance with EN45012 and that its assessors are educated, trained and experienced to levels equivalent to those expected of own staff.

Each of the signatories of the bi-lateral agreement agrees to promote, to the best of its ability, the acceptability and use by customers of any organisation, whose quality system has been certified by either party. If requested by a certified organisation, the following statements of equivalence can be added to the appendix of certificates:

> for BSI QA: According to the agreement between BSI and
>   (insert name of other party) dated (insert
>   date) it is hereby confirmed that this BSI
>   Certificate is equivalent to a (insert name of
>   other party) certificate.

or vice versa: for the other party.

However, recognising the need many organisations have for obtaining certification in counties other than their own, the parties will cooperate to provide the most effective service to applicants.

Agreements to date have been signed with the following certification bodies in EQNET.

DS   -   Dansk Standardisenings rad - Denmark

DQS   -   Deutsche Gesellschaft zur
           zertifizierung Qualitatssiche
           vungs systemen mbh - Germany

SIS   -   Standardissenings kommissioinen -
           i Sverige

SQS   -   Schweizerische Vereinigung fuer
           Qualitatssioherungs - Zertifikate - Switzerland

THE WORLD SCENE - MoU

For countries within the rest of the world, the bi-lateral agreements are further developed into Memorandum of Understanding (MoU).

Certificates are issued by both Certification Bodies following a successful assessment against the ISO9000 series, in which only one body may have participated.

Certificates produced against a MoU are, by prior arrangement between the client and Certifying bodies, issued jointly. The procedure is not automatic, and a client must declare his intention at the time of application to both parties. Certificates are not issued retrospectively, and statements of equivalence are not permitted on Certificates.

Issues of a Certificate following a UL assessment, for example, may be accompanied by the simultaneous issue of a BSI Certificate, even though BSI has not been represented at the assessment. Reciprocal arrangements apply equally.

Bi-lateral agreements and MoU's are achieved by the implementation of a programme of mutual auditing, scrutiny of assessment and registration procedures, assessment reports and the monitoring of one Certification Body by another.

The MoU between UL and BSI was supported by activities which covered the training of UL assessors and familiarisation with each bodies' procedures.

Reports issued after assessments are checked by each partner to verify that the assessment:

a) covered the ISO9000 Standard for which the applicant was seeking Certification.

b) covered the scope of Certification required by the client at the site assessed.

Further evidence may be required if all the above information is not available.

Following Registration, the first surveillance visit following BSI or UL Certification will be conducted jointly. Thereafter, one surveillance visit every two years must be conducted jointly.

MoU's to date has been developed and implemented with UL - Underwriters Laboratory - USA.

MoU's without developed implementation programmes have been signed with the following organisations:

Japanese Machinery and Metals Inspection Institute	Japan
Quality Management Institute (QMI) Covers quality management assessment only	Canada
Singapore Institute of Standards and Industrial Research (SISIR)	Singapore
SISIR and the Construction Industry Development Board (CIDB) (A three-party MoU)	Singapore
Testing Laboratory Registration Council (TELARC)	New Zealand

CONCLUSION

Working with a framework, by experienced and practising industrialists from countries all over the world will keep the Chemical Industry in the Vanguard of industries with the high quality range.

ACCREDITED CERTIFICATION BODIES
(as at 31 May 1990)

Certification Body	Reg No	Date of	Accreditation Cat.	Scope
Associated Offices Quality Certification Longridge House Longridge Place Manchester M60 4DT Tel 061 833 2295	014	May 1990	1	Annex 1
ASTA Certification Services Prudential Chambers 23/24 Market Place Rugby CV21 3DU Tel 0788 578435	010	Jun 1989	1	Annex 2
BSI Quality Assurance PO Box 375 Milton Keynes MK14 6LL Tel 0908 220908	003	Jan 1987	1 & 2	Annex 3
British Approvals Service for Electric Cables Silbury Court 360 Silbury Boulevard Milton Keynes MK9 2AF Tel 0908 691121	004	Apr 1987	1	Annex 4
Bureau Veritas Quality International Ltd 3rd floor 70 Borough High St London SE1 1XF Tel 071 378 8113	008	Nov 1988	1	Annex 5
Ceramic Industry Certification Scheme Ltd Queens Road, Penkhull Stoke on Trent ST4 7LQ Tel 0782 411008	006	Jul 1987	1 & 2	Annex 6
Construction Quality Assurance Arcade Chambers The Arcade, Market Place Newark Notts N24 1UD Tel 0636 708700	012	Jul 1987	1	Annex 7
Detnorske Veritas Quality Assurance Ltd Veritas House 112 Station Rd Sidcup Kent DA15 7BU Tel 081 309 7477	013	Jul 1989	1	Annex 8

ACCREDITED CERTIFICATION BODIES
(as at 31 May 1990)

Certification Body	Reg No	Accreditation Date of	Cat.	Scope
Lloyd's Register Quality Assurance Ltd Norfolk House Wellesley Rd Croydon CR9 2DT Tel 081 688 6882 081 688 6883	001	Feb 1986	1	Annex 9
The Loss Prevention Certification Board Ltd Melrose Ave Boreham Wood Hertfordshire WD6 2BJ Tel 081 207 2345	007	Oct 1988	1 & 2	Annex 10
The Quality Scheme for Ready Mixed Concrete 3 High Street Hampton Essex TW12 2SQ Tel 081 941 0273	009	Dec 1988	2	Annex 11
SIRA Certification Service Saighton Lane Saighhton Chester CH3 6EG Tel 0244 332200	011	Jun 1989	1 & 2	Annex 12
UK Certificatiion Authority for Reinforcing Steels Oak House, Tube Hill Sevenoaks Kent TN13 1BL Tel 0732 450000	002	Oct 1986	1 & 2	Annex 13
Yarsley Quality Assured Firms Ltd Trowers Way Redhill RH1 2JN Tel 0737 768445	005	Apr 1987	1	Annex 14

Subject Index

DATE DUE

APR 12 1993